Mount Kenya

The summit peaks, Batian and Nelion, swathed in evening cloud.

JOHN READER

Mount Kenya

ELM TREE BOOKS

LONDON

ELM TREE BOOKS
Published by the Penguin Group
27 Wrights Lane, London W8 5TZ, England
Viking Penguin Inc., 40 West 23rd Street, New York, New York 10010, U.S.A.
Penguin Books Australia Ltd, Ringwood, Victoria, Australia
Penguin Books Canada Ltd, 2801 John Street, Markham, Ontario, Canada L3R 1B4
Penguin Books (N.Z.) Ltd, 182–190 Wairau Road, Auckland 10, New Zealand
Penguin Books Ltd, Registered Offices: Harmondsworth, Middlesex, England

First Published in Great Britain 1989 by Elm Tree Books
Text and photographs copyright © 1989 by John Reader

British Library Cataloguing in Publication Data

Reader, John, *1937*–
 Mount Kenya.
 1. Kenya. Mount Kenya
 I. Title

916.76'24

ISBN 0–241–12486–7

Designed by Peter Campbell

Map by Chapman and Bounford

Produced by Mandarin Offset in Hong Kong

Contents

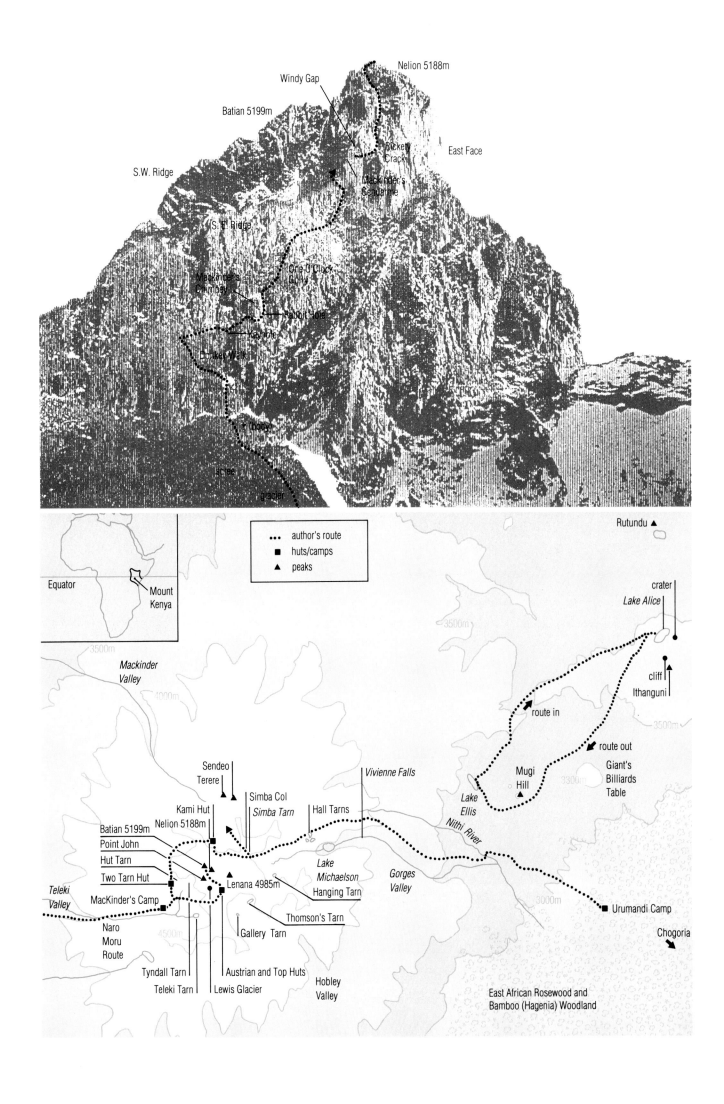

Nelion 5188m

Windy Gap

Batian 5199m

Bickett Crack

East Face

S.W. Ridge

Mackinder's Gendarme

S.E. Ridge

One O'Clock Gully

Mackinder's Chimney

Rabbit Hole

Keyhole

Donkey Walk

Y (body)

scree

glacier

Equator

Mount Kenya

········ author's route

■ huts/camps

▲ peaks

Rutundu ▲

crater
Lake Alice

3500m

Mackinder Valley

4000m

cliff

Ithanguni

route in

3500m

route out

Giant's Billiards Table

Sendeo

Terere

Simba Col

Simba Tarn

Vivienne Falls

Hall Tarns

Mugi Hill

Lake Ellis

Nithi River

3300m

Kami Hut

Nelion 5188m

Batian 5199m

Point John

Hut Tarn

Two Tarn Hut

MacKinder's Camp

Teleki Valley

Lenana 4985m

Lake Michaelson

Hanging Tarn

Gorges Valley

3000m

Urumandi Camp

Naro Moru Route

4500m

Thomson's Tarn

Gallery Tarn

Chogoria

Tyndall Tarn

Austrian and Top Huts

Teleki Tarn

Lewis Glacier

Hobley Valley

East African Rosewood and Bamboo (Hagenia) Woodland

CHAPTER ONE

Facing the Mountain

My daughter gave me a bible for my 50th birthday, enclosing with the gift a piece of paper on which she had written the words: 'a book no practising atheist should be without...' At Christmas that year I showed her a photograph of a climber on the north east face of Mount Kenya and she told me I was mad even to think of tackling that route. By the time I got to the summit a few weeks later, my memories of the birthday gift and the Christmas admonishment had become inseparable – each reminded me of the other. I did not take the bible with me, but there were moments on the mountain when a belief in its capacity to inspire, uplift and sustain would have been deeply comforting.

The atheism I practise is not so much a denial of the efficacy of religious belief as an insistence that beliefs of any kind serve a functional purpose in human affairs. The revered status of Mount Kenya in the affairs of the Kikuyu people is a case in point. The Kikuyu are farmers living on the foothills of the mountain and its adjacent highlands – all good arable land. The name Kenya is a corruption of the Kikuyu name for the mountain, Kirinyaga, meaning mountain of brightness. The Kikuyu believe that their God, Ngai, the Lord of Nature, resides on the peak. They have a creation myth which tells how Ngai carried the first man, Gikuyu, to the summit and commanded him to make his home in a grove of fig trees at the heart of the fertile land below. Lo and behold, when Gikuyu reached the grove he found a beautiful wife awaiting his pleasure. Her name was Mumbi, meaning creator or moulder. Mumbi and Gikuyu had nine daughters, for whom Ngai magically provided nine strong and handsome young men when Gikuyu pointed out that his daughters must have husbands if the family line was to thrive. In due course, the nine couples founded the nine clans of the Kikuyu.

But Ngai had demanded a gesture of obeisance before supplying the nine young men. Gikuyu had been instructed to kill a lamb and a kid from his flock, and burn the meat as an offering to his benefactor. This had been done at the foot of the largest fig tree in the grove, facing Mount Kenya.

In due course, the Kikuyu have become the largest and most powerful tribal group in Kenya. Very few today would claim that the story of Gikuyu and Mumbi is factually true, but none would deny that a shared belief in the efficacy of prayer and ritual sacrifice has been a very important factor in the growth and success of the Kikuyu. Traditionally, each major event in the life of the individual, the family, and the community had to be accompanied by a sacrificial offering and prayers to Ngai. The Kikuyu believed that no homestead could be established successfully, or marriage contracted, or field planted, or crop harvested, or elder elected without the appropriate prayer and ceremony. The supplicants assembled under the sacred tree and directed their offerings and prayers towards Ngai on his altar – Kirinyaga. They spread their arms, lifted their faces towards the mountain, and prayed. Thus the term, facing Mount Kenya, acquired a very special meaning for the Kikuyu – a fact of which Jomo Kenyatta was surely well aware when he chose it as the title of the book on the Kikuyu he published in 1938.

In *Facing Mount Kenya* Kenyatta gives some very persuasive examples of the power of belief in Kikuyu affairs. One passage tells of the solemn appeals that were made to Ngai in times of drought. With offerings of lamb, honey-beer and milk, the elders would gather beneath the sacred tree facing Mount Kenya and plead: 'You who make mountains tremble and rivers flood; we offer to you this sacrifice that you may bring us rain. People and children are crying; flocks and herds are crying. ... We beseech you to accept this, our sacrifice, and bring us rain of prosperity.' And the people would respond: 'Peace, we beseech you, Ngai, peace be with us.'

Of a rain ceremony in which he took part as a child, Kenyatta reports: 'Our prayers were quickly answered, for even before the sacred fires had ceased to burn, torrential rain came upon us. We were soaked, and it will not be easy for me to forget the walk home in the downpour.' Kenyatta saw other ceremonies for rain as he grew older and in *Facing Mount Kenya* states categorically that: 'Every rain ceremony that I have witnessed has been very soon followed by rain.'

Kenyatta was a major figure in Kenya's independence movement, and when he became the first president of the country in December 1963 he drew the nation around him, facing Mount Kenya.

From a functional point of view, the Kikuyu belief in the efficacy of the prayers they offered to Ngai on Mount Kenya can be attributed to a very sensible realisation that the mountain is the source of the land and the rain upon which their lives depend. The soil is particularly fertile by virtue of its volcanic origin and the accumulation of humus produced by the forest, and the bulk of the mountain deflects the seasonal monsoons upward as they blow in from the Indian Ocean and thus causes rain to fall on the mountain foothills and immediate surroundings. Belief in a supernatural origin of factors so crucial to the success of agricultural endeavour instilled respect. Furthermore, such beliefs made everyone subject to the same transcendental authority. No one could escape the rule of Ngai, and thus the ambitions of the individual were always subject to the rule of the group.

All this made sense, and even the national fervour which united Kenyans behind their leaders at independence could be attributed to the primary significance of Mount Kenya in national affairs, for the majority of the country's population lives either close to the mountain or on the highlands geologically associated with it. But an historical puzzle remained. If Kirinyaga was the sacred mountain of the Kikuyu, why had its peaks been given Maasai names?

Relations between the Maasai and the Kikuyu are generally reckoned to epitomize the ancient antipathy which has always kept nomadic pastoralist and sedentary agriculturalist apart. The Kikuyu name for the Maasai, *Ugabi*, also means enemy, and yet the peaks of their sacred mountain have been named Batian, Nelion, Sendeyo and Terere after Maasai leaders who are said to have been the scourge of the Kikuyu. Early historical accounts described the Kikuyu as industrious and peaceful, but the Maasai were said to love war, slaughter, looting and rape. Two overriding passions – cattle and warfare – ruled their lives. Perpetual warfare distinguished the Maasai's relationship with the Kikuyu, an observer reported at the turn of the century.

Like most European visitors to Kenya, I accepted this description of tribal relations in Kenya unquestioningly. Though well aware that European accounts of African history are often self-serving, the story of longstanding animosity between Maasai and Kikuyu accorded with my own deep-seated assumption that human society has always been split into two basic groups: wanderers and settlers. And being a bit of a wanderer myself, imbued with the romantic fascination for open wild country which afflicts many urbanites, my sympathies lay with the

Maasai. On the basis of hardly any knowledge at all I assumed that they had driven their herds and flocks down the Rift Valley and on to the slopes of Mount Kenya long before the Kikuyu arrived on the scene. And when the Kikuyu came along, they took possession of the land which the Maasai stock had grazed freely; they tilled the ground, erected fences, built permanent settlements and even claimed Kirinyaga as the home of their God. No wonder there was animosity between the two groups – the nomadic and sedentary ways of life are fundamentally incompatible.

These assumptions were still unchallenged when I opened my newly acquired bible one evening and began to read from Genesis 4: 'And Abel was a keeper of sheep, but Cain was a tiller of the ground. ... and it came to pass, when they were in the field, that Cain rose up against Abel his brother, and slew him.'

A revelation! Here, I thought, was confirmation that the antagonism which lies between the sedentary and nomadic sections of society has been a recognized source of evil for a very long time. Furthermore, it was Cain, the farmer, who killed Abel, the herdsman. And the final irony, of course, was that Cain was banished from the garden of Eden for his crime and thereby forced to become a wanderer himself. The bible leaves no doubt about who was the guilty party, and thus even an atheist might infer that the Maasai have been more sinned against than sinning in their relationship with the Kikuyu.

On my way to the mountain I called on Godfrey Muriuki, Professor of History at the University of Nairobi and author of a very good book on the history of the Kikuyu. I had expected that he would be conversant with the functionalist approach to cultural matters, and was surprised that his answer to my questions about the role of Mount Kenya in Kikuyu affairs tended to place more emphasis on the importance of the mountain as a focus of ritual and ceremony, than on its functional significance. Believing that God resided on Mount Kenya certainly had exercised a cohesive influence on the Kikuyu, he said, but their reverence for the mountain simply filled a spiritual need which is common to all people.

The professor laughed when I revealed my unquestioning acceptance of the story that the Maasai and the Kikuyu were longstanding enemies. 'That is a fiction,' he said, 'invented by the colonial administration. There was sporadic fighting, yes, but the Kikuyu fought among themselves as much as they fought with the Maasai. Fact is, the Kikuyu traded with the Maasai, there was a good deal of exchange and intermarriage between them, fighting was in neither's interest. And look at the influence the Maasai had on the Kikuyu: important aspects of Kikuyu social and ritual practice are borrowed from the Maasai; the Kikuyu language is heavily indebted to Maasai, all the words relating to cattle, for instance, are taken from the Maasai ...'

Even the word for God is shared – Ngai in Kikuyu; Nkai, or E'Ngai in Maasai. But here there is an added twist, for while the Kikuyu Ngai refers only to their God, the Maasai use the word Nkai to describe both their deity and the natural phenomenon upon which their lives depend. Nkai means both God and rain to the Maasai. For them, speaking of one implies a prayer to the other, and there can hardly be a more functional link between the spiritual and secular aspects of life.

And the peaks of Kirinyaga, named Batian, Nelion and Lenana? I subsequently discovered that they had been given Maasai names in 1899 by Halford Mackinder, the first man to reach the summit of the mountain, at the suggestion of the District Officer for Maasailand, who had been particularly helpful when Mackinder's expedition encountered problems with the

9

Kikuyu. The Maasai themselves call Mount Kenya *ol donyo eibor*, the white mountain, granting it no special reverence in their lives.

I lived in Nairobi from 1969 until 1978. At first, the heights I intended to climb were primarily of a professional nature. Photo-journalism was my job and I had a contract with *Life* magazine to cover Africa south of the Sahara from the Time-Life office in Nairobi.

Life had pioneered the concept of the photo-essay and the illustrated magazine story in the 1930s, closely followed by *Picture Post* in England. I remember turning the pages of *Picture Post* as a child in the years immediately after the war, hoping, hoping they would contain some pictures of animals or adventure. Often enough they did. *Picture Post* faded during the early fifties and finally folded in 1957 but *Life* grew in stature. Those large, gritty, unequivocal images left an indelible impression – so much more real than the glossy prettiness of *National Geographic*. Picture essays by Eugene Smith and George Silk in particular broadened my vision of what was possible. Their achievements seemed so fantastic, and *Life* magazine soon towered high above any other target that my ambitions might aspire to.

By 1969 I had established a firm foothold on the slopes of the trade, the summit was in sight and the contract with *Life* offered a route to the top. I rented a small cottage on a dairy and coffee farm a few kilometres north of Nairobi, more than 2000m above sea level. The cottage was built of dressed lava stone, floored with cedar blocks, and the roof was open to the rafters. The evenings could be chilly, so we regularly made a fire of old coffee stumps in the grate. Trees and shrubs surrounded the cottage – jacaranda blossom dusted the lawn from October to January; bamboo waved above the carport; poinsettia, dahlias and roses flourished in the patch of ground where the bathwater soaked away; a cuckoo regularly parasitized the robinchats who nested in the flowering creeper.

The view from the bedroom window was dominated by a monkey puzzle tree (whose resinous branches fell regularly enough to provide a steady supply of firelighters), but on clear mornings we could see the glistening peaks of Mount Kenya, 120km away, rising above the intervening ridges of coffee plantation and forest like the whitened spires of some improbable cathedral. On those mornings we knew that we would be able to see Kilimanjaro too, as we drove down through Banana Hill towards Nairobi. When I moved to Kenya in 1969 you could see both mountains with a turn of the head from Time-Life's tenth floor offices on a clear day – Kilimanjaro to the south, Kenya to the north. That view spanned over 300km. It's no longer visible – obliterated not only by higher buildings, but also by the smoggy air of a growing city.

The first three years in Africa were intended to be a probationary assignment, and during 1972 I began petitioning for a move to *Life's* New York office. And then they closed down the magazine. Or 'suspended publication', as it was phrased in the message of 12 December 1972 (the magazine started up again as a monthly in 1978, but has never regained its former stature). I remember my reaction to the announcement vividly: numbness and chagrin. It was hard to believe that just as I was poised for an assault on the summit, the mountain itself had crumbled beneath me. I resumed full freelance status; and Africa proved a good place to be.

We kept the cottage as our base. The chart in the kitchen recorded that our hens laid 1284 eggs in 1976, but we can have eaten very few of them. We were away more often than we were at home. Finally, in 1978 we moved to England, though Africa remained a central focus of interest.

In 1974 I accompanied a group of American students to the summit of Lenana on Mount Kenya for a magazine story, and in 1979 I spent several weeks on Kilimanjaro. The latter was a memorable experience which provided the raw material for a book. I thought it made quite a good book, and a number of friends and reviewers seemed to agree – but with one notable exception. Iain Allan reviewed the book for *Swara*, a magazine published by the East African Wildlife Society, and was scathing. Evidently he considered my offering pretty poor stuff. While I had thought it amusing to mention that the world's highest tiddlywinks competition had been played on the summit, he thought I should have given more attention to Mawenzi (a formidable heap of fractured rock which constitutes the second highest peak on the massif); while I thought my own experiences were interesting enough to relate, he said I should have written of more notable climbs and climbers.

But then Iain Allan is a climber himself; furthermore, he is a world-famed expert on the mountains of East Africa, where he has pioneered many hair-raising routes. He is also a writer, and the sheer vehemence of his review strongly suggested that I had preempted his own plans for a book on Kilimanjaro. This was a consoling thought. No one likes to be preempted, any more than they welcome scathing reviews; but Iain Allan's book would be very different from mine. So different, in fact, that there should be room for both in the bookshops. It seemed to me that we ought to meet and talk about it some day, and I rather relished the prospect. Perhaps he would be kind enough to tell me how to go about writing a book on Mount Kenya.

Iain Allan founded a safari company called Tropical Ice. It is a select and very successful operation which specializes, as the name implies, in taking enthusiasts high above the snowline on the East African mountains. Though the company also offers less demanding safaris, Iain Allan likes nothing better than taking people on challenging climbs. His typical relaxing weekend might include several hours of clinging to a rockface in danger of multiple fractures should he fall. Now that Tropical Ice is so successful, however, most of its safaris are led by the company's other guides, and a typical working week for Iain Allan includes many hours of sitting behind a desk on the fifth floor of an office building in Nairobi.

That was where I found him. The receptionist said I should go straight into his private office. Iain was seated at his desk, back to the window, pen in hand, surrounded by papers. He is a large man, and the office seemed marginally too small for him. Maps and a large chart of safari schedules hung on two walls; photographs of lions attacking and demolishing some very lifelike human models were prominent on a third. Iain stood up and began to put out his hand as I introduced myself. He hesitated as the name registered and for a moment was wonderfully discommoded. He actually blushed, and then began to laugh. We both laughed.

I enjoyed the meeting enormously, and the enjoyment was substantially enhanced when Iain revealed the coincidental nature of the moment. Right there and then he was completing a chapter on Kilimanjaro for Clive Ward's book of photographs on the mountains of East Africa. My book had been very helpful, he said. Charitably, and perhaps also a little contritely, he went on to say that until he had begun to work on the text for Clive's book, he had not realized that books were so much more difficult to write than book reviews. Well, a statement like that speaks volumes.

Writers who climb and climbers who write are certain to approach identical mountains from quite different points of view, but Iain and I established the common ground of friendship in his office that morning. I asked him about Mount Kenya. Go up the Chogoria route on the east side of the mountain, he suggested. Call on Livingstone Barine if you need guides or porters. He endorsed my plans to spend some days alone on the mountain, and suggested I should explore the Gorges Valley, as well as the little-known eastern shoulder of the mountain, where Lake Alice lies hidden (I was particularly taken with this idea, since Alice is the name of my youngest daughter).

And when I mentioned that I wanted to attempt a climb on the summit, he offered to take me. 'I'll get you up there,' he said. But I felt bound to reveal the limits of my climbing experience: I have scrambled about on several mountains, but never with ropes on what mountaineers call serious rock climbs. He looked me straight in the eye for a moment, then asked: 'Are you afraid of heights, sheer drops, that sort of thing?'

I recalled a childhood experience of crawling, terrified, around the wall of the whispering gallery, high in the dome of St. Paul's Cathedral, but hoped that the intervening decades had left me more able to deal with such things.

'No, I don't believe so,' I replied.

'Right, then let's fix a date,' he said.

The twin peaks of the summit, Nelion and Batian, seen through a cleft in the Gorges Valley.

Evening cloud slips down the Mackinder Valley below the mountain's subsidiary
peaks - Terere (4714m) and Sendeyo (4704m).

The summit peaks from the south-west. Batian and Nelion with the Diamond Glacier
and Couloir on the left; Point John (4883m), right.

From the summit of
Nelion, looking south-
west down the
Teleki Valley;
Point John on the left,
Tyndall Tarn and Hut
Tarn, right.

There are 32 tarns on Mount Kenya. Hanging Tarn lies at 4400m at the head of the Gorges Valley.

At 4900m, traversing the south face of Nelion, above the Darwin Glacier (lower right).

The south ridge at
sunset from Top Hut.
Point John (left),
Batian and Nelion (right)
loom above the Lewis
Glacier (foreground).

Gallery Tarn (left) and Thompson's Tarns (right), with the
Hobley Valley descending to the forest beyond.

From the summit of Nelion, looking north down Mackinder Valley. The peaks
Terere and Sendeyo in the middle distance.

Shadowy glimpses of the north summit ridge, through evening cloud from Kami Hut.

CHAPTER TWO

Beginnings

Africa – the very name has a sound to it that tugs at the soul of urban wanderers like me. Say it aloud, and the three syllables resonate in the throat like a cry from before the beginnings of speech. The name has no sharp corners, no explosive T or hissing S; it is welcomingly smooth and rounded, like the continent itself.

Ex Africa semper aliquid novi – from Africa there is always something new, the Romans declared. They knew the continent only so far as civilization had extended up the Nile, but they marvelled at the treasures and wonders that adventurous traders brought back from their encounters with the people who inhabited the lands beyond – gold, precious stones, ivory, elephants, the giraffe, the rhinoceros …

And before the Romans, Queen Hatshepsut had sent expeditions to the Land of Punt (Eritrea and northern Somalia) which returned with myrrh, ebony, ivory, gold, cinnamon, skins, live monkeys, slaves … The Carthaginians had sailed down the west coast, the Greeks had sailed from the Red Sea and south of the Horn of Africa. Early in the Christian era, Indian and Chinese vessels established trading links with towns along the east coast. The Arabs followed, then the Portuguese, the British, the French, Germans and Dutch. They were all looking for something new, and for centuries, Africa always seemed able to fulfil its tantalizing promise.

But even as late as the 19th century, maps of Africa still showed the central area of the continent as a blank space, labelled 'parts unknown'. The coastline had been precisely survey-ed; the coastal towns were well known, and some inland parts had been explored, but the interior remained another world, awaiting discovery. It was of course disease (principally malaria) that thwarted the explorers – disease and the fact that Africans had no wish, and certainly no need to involve outsiders with their internal affairs. But those deterrents were overcome towards the end of the 19th century by the combined effect of quinine and colonial ambition. Fast on the heels of adventurous explorers, the colonial powers carved up the contin-ent into 'spheres of influence', and tied each one to a European economy. Sources of cheap raw materials for industry were exploited, and profitable markets for industrial output established.

During the 20th century, knowledge has been prominent among the new treasures which have come from Africa. Knowledge which has revealed, paradoxically, that Africa was never new to mankind, for we originated there. Furthermore, the continent was at the very heart of the landmass, Pangaea, on which terrestrial life itself began 350 million years ago. The earliest-known mammals were tiny shrew-like creatures which scurried about in the shadows of dino-saurs in southern Africa about 200 million years ago. The ancestral ape lived in east Africa around 20 million years ago, and one of its several descendents, the ancestor of man, *Australo-pithecus*, appeared on the plains of east Africa 3.5 million years ago, before even Kilimanjaro and Mount Kenya had begun to erupt from the fractures that created the Rift Valley.

This new information has come to light in the past 25 years, courtesy of the fossils that have been found throughout Africa. Numerous skulls, teeth and skeletal remains have been unearth-ed, but the most evocative evidence of human ancestry is a trail of footprints left by a group of three hominids as they strode across a mudpan at Laetoli, in what is now southern Tanzania, 3.6 million years ago. Their feet sank a few centimetres into the mud; one of them walked directly in the footsteps of the largest individual, pace by pace. The smallest of the three seems to have stopped half way across, when he or she turned to the left, perhaps to glance back at Lemagrut, the volcano then showering the landscape with the ash in which the footsteps were preserved.

The delicate hominid trail at Laetoli was preserved along with numerous tracks of antelope, baboons, birds, giraffe, rhinos, elephants and hyenas. Ancestors, so long ago, but what frail figures they must have been. They stood barely 150cm high, they were lightly built and, one might think, not at all well-equipped for survival among the animals of the day. None could run as fast as a gazelle, or slice up raw meat as readily as a hyena; they were not equipped to climb trees with the ease of a baboon, or swim as well as a crocodile and, if modern humans are anything to go by, an eagle could see better, an elephant could smell more keenly, and even a fly had a more highly developed sense of taste than our ancestors.

But the ancestors stood erect, their hands were free to develop manipulative skills and, above all, they possessed one special characteristic which was destined to set their descendents apart from all other animals – a brain with the potential capacity to reason. The brain enabled them to anticipate the actions of other animals, to recognize and seize opportunities as they arose, and to avert danger before it struck. With these talents our early ancestors were able to exploit every niche the African cradleland had to offer; thus their descendents have populated the globe. Only the cockroach is more widespread.

The first evidence of man's African origin to be recognized was a fossil skull which came into the hands of the anatomist Raymond Dart in 1924. The fossil had been found during the course of lime-quarrying operations at Taung, on the edge of the Kalahari in South Africa. It consisted of the face and jaw of a child, together with a cast of the brain which fitted snugly behind the forehead. When Dart reported his findings in the pages of *Nature* the following year, he named the specimen *Australopithecus africanus*, meaning the southern ape of Africa, though he was certain that it represented the earliest known ancestor of man.

A. africanus is a tiny, exquisite and evocative fossil – certainly one of the world's great treasures. The jaw, with its crowded molars and peg-like incisors, is very much like that of a modern child aged about six or seven. But the face is distinctly ape-like. The cheekbones are high, the eye sockets circular and close together, and the jaw juts forward. The brain was no larger than might be found in an ape of that size, but Dart had made a special study of the anatomy of the brain, and the braincast of the Taung child revealed to him features that were more human than ape-like. The pattern of convolutions and fissures at the rear of the Taung brain were distinctly human in their configuration, he said. Furthermore, the spinal cord had joined the brain through the base of the skull, indicating that the head had been balanced on the top of the spine, as is characteristic of man, not slung forward like that of the apes. Therefore *Australopithecus* had walked erect and stood very close to the beginnings of man's evolutionary path, Dart concluded.

But Dart's claims contradicted prevailing ideas about the early ancestry of mankind and were largely dismissed until the 1950s, by which time Robert Broom, a crusty Scots doctor of medicine and science, had found further quantities of australopithecine fossils in the South African cave sites. These included parts of the skeleton which confirmed the upright stance of the australopithecines, and skulls which confirmed the ape-like proportions of their brains. Clearly, the australopithecines possessed a mixture of man- and ape-like characteristics.

Since the 1960s, many more fossils have been recovered from excavations in East Africa, including a number of australopithecines. A new species has been named to describe the oldest of these: *Australopithecus afarensis*. Most of the *A. afarensis* specimens have come from the Afar Depression in Ethiopia, but some have also been found in deposits near the footprint trail at Laetoli, in Tanzania, which have been dated at 3.6 million years old.

The brain of *A. afarensis* is small, the face juts forward, and the arms are as long as those of a chimpanzee, but the configuration of the teeth is human, and the stance no different from that of modern humans. Most authorities now believe that the trail of footprints at Laetoli were probably made by *A. afarensis* and that this marks the beginnings of humanity.

Like random signposts on an abandoned trail, the fossils provide tantalizing clues to the early course of human evolution in Africa. *Homo habilis* marks the moment around 2 million years ago when stone tools and technology began to affect human affairs (hence the name *Homo habilis*, meaning 'handy man'). Next comes *Homo erectus*, the most widely dispersed and longest surviving of the fossil hominids, who first appeared in east Africa about 1.6 million years ago, and subsequently spread across the continent and throughout the old world from Europe to the Far East, where the youngest of them dates from about 200,000 years ago.

Neanderthal Man is thought to have evolved from *Homo erectus* in Europe and western Asia, while back in the cradleland of east and southern Africa the essentially modern form of man was emerging. *Homo sapiens* was widely dispersed throughout the continent by 100,000 years ago, and some had already moved out of the continent, across the isthmus of Suez into the Middle East. Successive generations of the migrants' offspring spread around the world, displacing or interbreeding with the previously established populations as they advanced. They reached Europe between 55,000 and 28,000 years ago, Asia by 53,000 years ago and crossed the Bering Straits landbridge into the Americas sometime after 20,000 years ago. According to this scheme of things the entire world was populated by the progeny of modern humans from Africa in little more than 100,000 years. Thus, we are all much more closely related than the diversity of looks, lifestyle and language might suggest. In fact, genetic studies have shown that a man from Birmingham and a woman from Papua New Guinea have as much in common as two Nigerians living in the same town, and the Kikuyu farmer is no less close to the Maasai herdsmen.

The implications of these findings are astounding: they mean that we are all descended from a small group of people who lived in the African cradleland just a flicker of evolutionary time ago. Mount Kenya was already an extinct volcano when modern humans first gazed upon it; the character of the modern landscape was already formed, and many of the plants and wild animals which it supported would be familiar to the people who live there today.

The fossils which testify to our ancestors' presence in East Africa over 3 million years ago are impressive, even beautiful. And so rare, representing no more than one individual in every 100 million that lived during the course of human evolution. But they offer only a very narrow glimpse of humanity. You look at the bones, the empty eye sockets, the worn teeth, and feel a sense of profound wonder that here are the actual physical remains of an individual who lived so long ago. But they evoke very little of the empathy that one might expect to feel for such an ancient relative.

Paradoxically, it is the less direct evidence of our ancestors' existence which awakens most fellow feeling. The footprints at Laetoli, for instance, provide a far greater sense of the individual predicament than any piece of fossil bone. And the same with stone tools. You pick up a tool, heft it, and immediately begin to think of the person who made and once used it. Was that person a man or a woman? A mother with children? A man alone? Were they hungry? You begin to wonder if the tool had been lost or simply discarded, and how long it had lain untouched before you found it. You know that the hand which first used the tool was identical to your own, and then, holding that piece of worked stone, turning it, running a thumb along the cutting edge, you suddenly realize that the experience is akin to shaking hands.

Yes, it is the evidence of everyday life, not the physical remains of the people themselves, which arouses the strongest sense of association with the burgeoning humanity of our earliest ancestors. Stone tools, pottery, metalwork, ruins, sculpture, and painting – these are the things which tell the story; and the story begins at Olduvai Gorge, a few days' walk from Mount Kenya.

A lake some ten kilometres long and five kilometres wide filled the Olduvai basin two million years ago, and it persisted for several hundred thousand years, despite the showers of volcanic ash with which it was inundated from time to time by nearby volcanoes. The lake was fed by numerous streams and small rivers flowing from the highlands, and was exceptionally rich in fish and bird life. However, geological faulting associated with the formation of the Rift Valley (and climatic changes) reduced the lake to about one-third of its original size by 1.6 million years ago, and by 1.2 million years ago it was nothing more than a series of seasonal pans dotted about an alluvial plain. The faulting not only drained the lake, but also altered the pattern of streams draining into the basin, ultimately concentrating their waters in a single large river which flowed from west to east. This river began cutting through the basin about half a million years ago, revealing the layer-cake pattern of deposits with which the basin had filled, and creating the gorge itself. Volcanoes continued to spew ash into the basin, and sediments continued to accumulate, so that the deposits cover a total of close on two million years. Olduvai Gorge is thus the longest, fullest and most revealing record of early man and his way of life yet found.

The major part of the investigations at Olduvai have been conducted by Louis and Mary Leakey. Louis first visited the Gorge in 1931, and Mary finally left it in 1984. During that span of more than half a century, 127 sites bearing evidence of early man were located along the length and breadth of the Gorge and throughout the geological sequence. Tens of thousands of artefacts and fossils were recovered, including massive stone anvils and tiny fish scales so perfectly fossilized that even their transparency is preserved.

The oldest tools found at Olduvai, dating from just under two million years ago, are water-worn cobbles from which a number of flakes had been chipped to form a sharp edge at one end. The result is more of a chopper than a cutting tool, but there seem to have been about six different types – sharp flakes for cutting skin and sinews, choppers for pounding meat and bone, scrapers for removing the scraps – and these tools are thought to be the basic butchering outfit which marked the human ancestors' transition from a predominantly vegetarian diet to one which included an increasingly large proportion of meat.

Until then, vegetable foods probably had constituted the major part of the hominid diet. No doubt they scavenged meat from carcasses abandoned by carnivores whenever the opportunity arose, but gathering would have been the occupation upon which their lives depended. The advent of stone tools changed all that. Tools opened the way to hunting and thus mark a significant development on the path of human evolution.

The growing importance of meat and stone tools in the life of early man is chronicled in the ascending sequence of sites at Olduvai. During the first 150,000 years, an increasing preponderance of large animals among the fossil bones is revealed, indicating that the skills needed to butcher large carcasses were acquired, and suggesting that the ancestors might even have been able to corner and kill the animals. The toolmakers also used a greater variety of stone as time passed, and travelled much further afield in search of their raw materials, which in turn suggests that the toolmakers were becoming aware that some types of stone produce better tools than others.

Most of the oldest tools found at Olduvai (on 1.8 million year old sites) were made of lava obtainable within 2km of the site, but tools made of other materials were found more frequently at sites from the 1 million year old deposits, and some were up to 10km from the nearest source of raw material. By 700,000 years ago the Olduvai basin was criss-crossed with a veritable network of supply routes. Tools made of gneiss, quartzite, trachyte and phonolite were carried up to 20km from their point of origin to the place where they were unearthed. Thus it is quite possible that some sort of trade in stone tools had developed by that time, long before trade had become a feature of life in any other part of the world.

Around 1.4 million years ago, a radically new tool arrived at Olduvai: a flat, pear-shaped implement, carefully flaked on both faces to form a cutting edge around the entire tool – the handaxe. The difference between the handaxe and pre-existing tools was primarily one of concept: whereas the older tools had been made from available cobbles and pieces of stone as found, the handaxes were made from large flakes which had been deliberately struck from a boulder. This practice created a core from which blanks of specific size and shape could be struck and flaked. Considerable skill was required, both in selecting the raw material and removing the flakes to best advantage.

Thus the first handaxe manufacturers must have worked to a preconceived plan, and their achievements mark a major step forward in the development of mankind's technological skill. The handaxe industry spread throughout Africa and Europe to become the foundation of stone tool technology world wide. The finest flint tools of the Stone Age, made around 6,000 years ago, were the end-product of basic techniques which had been developed in the East African cradleland of mankind more than one million years before.

It was the environment that inspired the innovation and the development of mankind's technological skills in East Africa. The cradleland was fertile and teemed with animal life. The region's carrying capacity is said to have been about ten times greater than that of the most favourable environments elsewhere, and such a vast resource could provide ample sustenance for the evolving human population. Under such circumstances, the incentive to develop advantageous hunting and gathering skills would have been considerable; population growth would have encouraged migration, and the migrants would have taken with them not only the skills of humanity to date, but also the ability to adapt those skills to different circumstances. Thus, the spread of the toolmakers was unremitting, throughout Africa and beyond.

The growth and dispersal of stone tool technology and people seems to have become particularly rapid from about 60,000 years ago, and by 35,000 years ago virtually every available ecological niche in Africa had been occupied. This relatively sudden proliferation of the human presence must indicate an equally rapid increase in the numbers of people on the continent, which, in turn, can only have resulted from a growing ability to find dependable food supplies in an ever greater variety of habitats. The cycle of interaction between environmental circumstances and the human talent for innovation was firmly established: environmental opportunities inspired innovations; innovations opened up yet more opportunities.

About 30,000 years ago, the toolmakers produced an innovation which was as important to the future of mankind as the first stone tool itself: the blade. Sharp, pointed and lethal, the blade exemplified the concept of the weapon in human affairs.

The blades were made by striking thin straight flakes from a carefully prepared core of fine-grained stone, one after another. This is a specialized technique which took a long time to arrive (after all, our ancestors had been making stone tools for nearly 2 million years before the blade appeared), but the technique enhanced the quality and usefulness of cutting tools beyond measure. Good knives, chisels, razors and gouges could be made to order, and tiny flakes of chalcedony, quartz, agate and chert were carefully fashioned into the barbs of harpoons, the teeth of saws, and the blades of wooden-handled knives, chisels and sickles. These were the first composite tools known to man.

The skill needed to make the barbs of a harpoon was only a flash of perception away from the techniques required to make the head of an arrow. With the triangular point lengthened, and notches chipped to the rear, a tang thus formed could be tied to the shaft with sinew or strips of skin. Small tanged points of this kind have been found at north African sites dating from before 12,000 years ago, and these are believed to be the first arrow-heads ever used, any-where.

Mankind was now firmly set in what is called the hunter-gatherer way of life, and doing rather well. The innovative talent which had carried our ancestors over the technological threshold, now developed into the utilitarianism which greatly increased their ability to occupy and exploit the diverse habitats of the Earth. By 10,000 years ago, people were widely distribut-ed throughout Africa and all parts of the world, excepting the extreme northern latitudes of Russia and Canada, and it is estimated that there were more than 10 million of them.

Though it was an innate ability to perceive opportunities and invent the means of exploiting them which fuelled our ancestors' progress along the evolutionary path to humanity, it was always the environment which determined the route, and the climate which set the pace. In East Africa, the land's rich store of plant and animal resources, and a lack of climatic extremes combined to provide the perfect cradleland for the early evolution of mankind. Being equator-ial, the region was not subjected to the extremes of climate which the Ice Ages brought to higher latitudes, but it experienced some amazing climatic changes none the less. Not changes of an order that would have threatened to eliminate the human line – no, the changes remained within the ecological constraints of early man's existence, but they altered the landscape decisively, and prompted the development of new talents.

At the height of the last major Ice Age about 18,000 years ago, when one-third of the earth's surface was covered with ice 1.6km thick on average, when the glaciers were barely a day's walk from where London now stands, and approaching the site of Pittsburgh in North

America, Africa was entering a period of steadily increasing heat and aridity. The effects were intense and widespread. By between 15,000 and 13,000 years ago, the equatorial forest had been reduced to a few relic patches in West Africa, and the Sahara had advanced 450km south of its present limit in some regions; Lake Victoria became an enclosed basin, no longer flowing into the Nile, and the White Nile itself dwindled to a seasonal trickle. Rainfall in the grasslands south of the Sahara is estimated to have been no more than 20 per cent of present-day levels during this period, but East Africa was less severely afflicted, receiving between 54 and 90 per cent of present-day rainfall – a factor which could only have intensified human activity in the cradleland.

Conditions became less arid from about 12,000 years ago. Over the next few millennia, average temperatures dropped and rainfall steadily increased. Between about 10,000 and 5,000 years ago, average rainfall in East Africa is estimated to have reached at least 165 per cent of present-day levels, while the Sahelian belt extending from the Sudan to Mauritania received up to four times more rain than it has in modern times. Once this heightened rainfall pattern had become established, its effect was dramatic. A broad swathe of dense equatorial forest extended across central Africa; some lowland forest advanced more than 400km north of its present limit, and much of the Saharan sand was converted to grassland and wooded savannah. In fact, the Sahara 'desert' is said to have existed only as a few relic patches of sand isolated by corridors of gallery forest and swamp during this period. Herds of elephant, giraffe and antelope roamed widely, and even hippos and crocodiles were commonplace in what is now the very heart of the desert.

By about 9,000 years ago, Africa was literally running with water. Streams and rivers flowed north and south from the mountains of the central Sahara; Lake Chad was far larger than the present day Lake Victoria (Africa's largest lake), and flowed to the Atlantic via the Benue River; Lake Victoria was twice as deep as it is today. In the East African cradleland, the soda lakes of present times were fresh with water running from the highlands; the surface of Lake Turkana in northern Kenya was 80 m above its present level, the lake covered more than 3,000 sq km of adjacent plains and repeatedly flowed over its north-western watershed and into the upper drainage of the White Nile.

So much water, teeming with fish. And the African hunters did not overlook the opportunities offered by this rich aquatic resource. A number of harpoons, beautifully carved from bone, have been found at a site to the north of Lake Turkana which dates from 9,100 years ago. These are the oldest harpoons known in Africa, and they mark the beginning of an aquatic culture which appears to have spread across the continent, from East Africa to the Atlantic, in the space of a few centuries. Around 8,000 years ago, fragments of pottery began to appear along with the harpoons, and these remnants of containers which were capable of holding liquid and withstanding heat, are believed to mark the 'fish stew' revolution, as one authority has so memorably described it.

The invention of the harpoon had enabled people to take advantage of a particularly rich resource, now pottery enabled them to cook it, and this happy conjunction established the significance of hearth and home in Africa. Thereafter, the waterside living sites show signs of increasingly long occupation. In all, more than fifty are known, extending in a broad band across Africa from Kenya to Mauritania. The earliest are those clustered around the shores of Lake Turkana.

When Africa's period of exceptional rains and cool temperatures began to draw to a close around 5,000 years ago, the falling water levels may have disadvantaged the fisherfolk settled on river banks and lake shores, but most can be expected to have adapted to the slowly changing circumstances, and some were perceptive enough to recognize the entirely new opportunities which the decline in rainfall offered. Sedimentary soils, rich in nutrients, had been deposited in the lake basins and river drainages during the wet period. The forests had receded again, leaving yet more expanses of rich soil. Grasses took root, transforming the newly exposed land into some of the finest pasture in Africa, and setting the scene for the next major development in the story of man in Africa – the move from hunting and gathering to the deliberate production of food.

CHAPTER THREE

Related Issues

Food production – the practice of growing crops and herding domesticated stock – was the fourth of the fundamental innovations which have added momentum to the course of human evolution. The process had begun nearly four million years ago, when our earliest ancestors literally stood up and walked away from their cousins to become gatherers; two million years ago they had begun fashioning stone tools and eventually had become hunters; more than 100,000 years ago the sapient line had emerged, and had spread out from Africa to inhabit the world; 10,000 years ago people began to produce their food, rather than simply hunt and gather it.

In effect, the shift from food gathering to food production transformed mankind from a passive beneficiary of the environment to its manipulator. Food production fostered the expansion of small settled communities into villages and then towns; it promoted the concept of private ownership, and it fuelled a population increase which continues to this day.

Food production began about 10,000 years ago with the selective cultivation of wild cereals and the domestication of wild sheep, goats and cattle in the crescent of fertile, well-watered soils which extended from the Mediterranean to Iraq, but its effects are most obvious in the Egyptian section of the Nile valley. It has been estimated that the valley probably supported no more than 20,000 hunters and gatherers 10,000 years ago, but the advent of food production increased its carrying capacity enormously, and within 2,000 years the valley was supporting a population of perhaps 5 million people in a habitable area the size of Belgium (which today supports just under 10 million people).

The unique fertility of the Nile valley is well-known. Rejuvenated each year with a flood of sediments from upstream, the land enabled the early Egyptian farmers to produce much more food than they required for their own domestic consumption. And it was this surplus which nurtured the religious and political systems of the Pharaonic Dynasties, and which fuelled the construction of their monuments. The achievements are staggering – the great pyramid at Giza, for instance, consists of 2.3 million blocks of stone, each weighing an average of 2.5 tonnes. The blocks were hewn, transported and set in place by human labour, and Herodotus reports that a labour force of 100,000 people worked for 20 years on the Giza pyramid. Thus while the monuments of ancient Egypt are applauded as examples of mankind's cultural achievement, they are also sombre memorials to the moment in the evolution of human affairs when the exploitation of the environment enabled people to exploit the labour of their fellows.

It might be supposed that the farming practised by the Egyptians would have spread inexorably southward, up the Nile into central Africa and onward even to the slopes of Mount Kenya. But this was not the case. The desert and the Nile swamps were formidable barriers, but more significantly, the Egyptian crops were not suited to the climatic conditions of the tropical and equatorial zones. Wheat and barley were adapted to the winter rainfall regime of the Mediterranean. Modern varieties do well on the highlands of Mount Kenya, but the first cultivated varieties would have failed even there. For this reason, it is probable that animal herding was the first aspect of food production to reach Africa south of the Sahara, while farming would await the domestication of indigenous sub-Saharan crops.

Africa's domestic animals are generally thought to have been introduced from the Near East, though two indigenous species of wild cattle also could have been involved. Direct evidence is sparse, but the transition from hunting to herding in Africa appears to have begun sometime after 8,000 years ago with the gradual spread of goats and sheep along the Mediterranean coast from the Near East. The earliest evidence of domestic cattle in Africa has come from a cave in the mountains of northern Algeria, where their bones have been identified on a succession of levels dating from 6,500 to 4,300 years ago. In fact, the proportion of cattle bones increases from 7.3 per cent to 24.7 per cent during the span of 2,200 years covered at the site, while the numbers of sheep and other animals decline. This increasing prevalence of cattle bones through time could be a unique record of domestication in progress, and some experts believe that the indigenous wild cattle of the Sahara probably were the source.

By 5,000 years ago the pastoralist way of life was common throughout the Sahara region from the Nile to the Niger. Hunters and gatherers also lived in the area, and fisherfolk were settled at lake shores and riversides, but pastoralism seems to have been the common denominator. The pottery and tools made by people throughout the region are all remarkably similar, which suggests that goods and ideas passed freely among the different groups.

Cattle bone has been found at a site dating from about 6,700 years ago in the Tassili mountains, in the depths of the Sahara, but the most compelling record of the people who herded their cattle across the rich pastures of what is now arid desert, is the work of hand and eye rather than the remains of man or beast. The desert is dotted from end to end with paintings and rock engravings. The outlines of animals are delicately pecked on flat rock surfaces; paintings in shades of soft ochre are preserved in rock shelters and caves.

These ancient images, faded but timeless, invite a person to stand precisely where others stood long before, and look at the world as they then saw it. The paintings depict wild animals such as buffalo, rhinoceros, hippopotamus, antelope and giraffe; herds of cattle also are shown, with their herders standing among them; and there are scenes of people hunting with bows, sitting beside their huts, and dancing.

The rock paintings confirm that people had lived in the Sahara region 5,000 years ago, but the effects of the climatic changes which had transformed the desert to well-watered parkland and drawn in the pastoralists were not all advantageous. Higher rainfall also encouraged the tsetse fly to advance into the Sahara region from the south, bringing sleeping sickness, trypano-somiasis, which can be fatal to people and cattle. The tsetse fly lives only in tropical wooded grassland which receives between 500mm and 700mm of rain each year, and as that rainfall regime broadened during Africa's pluvial period, so did the range of the tsetse. Of course, people and their animals all managed perfectly well in suitable regions where the rainfall was somewhat less than 500mm a year (even 250mm a year will support pastoralists provided there is water available for drinking), but the fly-belt which lay beyond the 500mm limit was an impenetrable barrier to their movement southward.

But the barrier was not stationary; it fluctuated with the climate, and as conditions in the Sahara became increasingly arid around 4,500 years ago, the fly-belt moved south to the very fringes of the equatorial forests. Pastoralists followed, winding down the watercourses which ran from the high ground of the central Sahara, and finally gaining access to a broad belt of savannah which lay between the increasingly inhospitable Sahara to the north, and the un-healthy equatorial regions to the south. This savannah is known today as the Sahel.

The Sahel, a belt of unsurpassed grassland up to 900km wide, stretching from the Atlantic in the west to the Ethiopian highlands in the east, might have been designed as a vast nursery and centre of diffusion for pastoralists in Africa. As in the Sahara, hunters and gatherers and fisherfolk were also present, and there seems to have been an extensive interchange of goods and skills between the different groups, but pastoralism was the foremost beneficiary of the environment. The Sahel nurtured the talents that pastoralists had developed to that time, and thus set in motion the cycles of population growth, migration, intermarriage and the exchange of ideas, which eventually carried the way of life to every suitable environment which the continent had to offer.

Pastoralists spread widely throughout the Sahel in a relatively short space of time. They reached the Ethiopian highlands before 4,000 years ago, and from there gained access to the corridor of open grassland which links the Sahel to the savannahs of central and southern Africa. Archaeological evidence from sites along the length of the Rift Valley records their presence at Lake Turkana about 2,500 years ago, whence they spread down past Nakuru, Naivasha and Mount Kenya to the open plains of southern Kenya and northern Tanzania.

The Maasai are the most recent and widespread inheritors of the pastoralist tradition in East Africa, though they have been present in the region as a distinct group only since between 1400 and 1600 AD. Maasai myths speak of their origin near Lake Turkana, where they occupied a crater-like depression surrounded by a steep escarpment. After a long period of drought, which had brought famine and despair, the elders noticed birds flying in with fresh green grass for their nests. Scouts climbed the treacherous cliffs of the escarpment to look for the source of the grass, and returned with news of a well-watered green and fertile land on the high ground beyond the crater. A huge ladder was built, and the people began to climb out of the crater with their cattle. Half of them had safely reached the high ground when the ladder broke, leaving the others no alternative but to remain behind. These people survived to leave the crater at a later date, when they became the forefathers of the Borana, Somali, Rendille, Pokot and other groups which occupy northern Kenya today.

Meanwhile, the ancestral Maasai advanced southward, displacing the semi-pastoral people who had previously occupied the grasslands. By the end of the 19th century the pastoral Maasai comprised a number of related Maa-speaking groups, and ranged across the Rift Valley grasslands from Marsabit in northern Kenya to Kiteto in southern Tanzania. At a conservative estimate, they probably totalled about 100,000 men, women and children at that time. By the 1980s, they had increased to more than 250,000, though their rangelands had been substantially decreased by European settlement, the creation of national game parks such as the Serengeti and Ngorongoro crater, and the encroachment of African agriculturalists such as the Kikuyu. These developments, along with the pressures of a cash economy, have made antagonism more obvious than mutual benefit in contemporary relations between the Maasai and their agriculturalist neighbours.

The advent and diffusion of pastoralism in Africa is relatively well recorded, but the same cannot be said of the other main thread of African food production – the domestication and cultivation of plants. This is not altogether surprising, for plant foods decay if they are not eaten, while bones stand at least some chance of being preserved. Grindstones testify to the preparation of foods, it is true, but the foods involved need not have been cultivated. Rock paintings might give a clue, but they record no scenes of people tilling the soil or harvesting a crop. Perhaps the paintings were made exclusively by hunters and herders; perhaps the farmers lacked suitable surfaces for any scenes they may have wished to paint; or perhaps they had less time or inclination for such activities. In any event, evidence of the beginnings of plant domestication in Africa south of the Sahara is slight. Direct evidence is extremely slight, amounting to a few seeds of cultivated millet found in association with pottery dating from between 5,000 and 4,000 years ago at a site in northern Ethiopia; and even this evidence is not unquestioned. The seeds seem so fresh, and their preservation so remarkable.

But if the direct evidence of the domestication of plants in sub-Saharan Africa is slight, possibly non-existent, the indirect evidence is substantial. Much of it is derived from the plants themselves.

While the cultivation of barley and wheat sustained vast numbers of people in the Nile valley, and subsequently spread across the Mediterranean to become the staple diet of the western world, Africa south of the Sahara was entirely dependent upon the cultivation of its own indigenous crops until the introduction of maize and cassava from the New World about 400 years ago, and rice and the banana from the Far East at some earlier but imprecise date. The indigenous crops were groundnuts, guinea rice and yams in West Africa; millets and sorghum throughout the Sahel; teff and the banana-like ensete in Ethiopia. And where were they domesticated? Along the fertile river beds and lake shores exposed as arid conditions returned to Africa some 5,000 years ago, it seems. By whom? The fisherfolk who had settled there.

These conclusions are derived from studies of the present distribution of the domesticated plants and their wild prototypes, coupled with consideration of the archaeological evidence and what is known of past climatic conditions. And the evidence is compelling. Indeed, independently produced maps showing the probable areas of initial domestication on the one hand, and of areas occupied by the early fishermen on the other, correlate exactly.

Though the indigenous domesticated plants of sub-Saharan Africa are nutritious and relatively easy to grow, they could not match the productivity of wheat and barley in the Nile valley. The land simply was not fertile enough; or rather, with nothing to match the flood of rejuvenating alluvium which the Nile laid over the fields each year, cultivated land elsewhere soon became impoverished. So the potential output of early sub-Saharan agriculture was limited, and the innovation did not fuel a population increase of the scale and momentum which the Nile valley experienced. Nor did it establish farming as a way of life which replaced all other means of satisfying the need for food. Farmers did not displace the hunters, fisherfolk and pastoralists. No, they co-existed. In fact, the groups became mutually dependent upon one another. Symbiotic ties were established as the farmers exchanged cultivated crops for game meat, fish and cattle produce, and the relationship which developed between the farmers and the pastoralists was particularly strong.

This was because the farmers not only needed cattle products, but also saw the value of the dung which the cattle deposited as they grazed down the stubble after the harvest. The pastoralists, for their part, appreciated the grazing reserve that the stubble and threshed stalks provided at the end of the dry season, and were glad to exchange meat and skins for a quantity of grain. Thus the two groups did not compete for resources, but each exploited different parts of the environment to the benefit of both, and once the African food plants had been domesticated, farming and pastoralism spread together through the Sahel and East Africa.

CHAPTER FOUR

Speaking of Which ...

If the potential for diversity carried in the genes of the modern humans who left Africa about 100,000 years ago could produce people as different in appearance as the Oslo urbanite and the New Guinea highlander in the course of 5,000 generations, one might expect that some degree of divergence must also have developed among the people who remained in Africa. And indeed it did, though the divergence is less obvious, simply because the greater part of the human population in Africa has never moved very far from the tropical cradleland in which mankind evolved.

Distinctive traits evolve in people as they adapt to the constraints of their environment. Similar environments elicit similar evolutionary traits, and thus Africans have remained broadly similar while the inhabitants of Scandinavia and New Guinea differ greatly.

Reproductive isolation of a viable breeding population is all that is required to establish distinctive traits. If a number of people occupy a particular territory to the exclusion of all others, and breed only among themselves, their progeny some generations later are likely to have a number of traits in common. These may be recognizable in the physique or physiognomy of individuals, but the distribution throughout the population is never total. Though the genes will create a general similarity of appearance, the inherent potential for diversity will always produce some individuals who look quite unlike even their closest relatives. Overall, there will always be a surprising amount of variation. In fact, in the final analysis there will be only one trait which is shared by absolutely all members of the population, and that, as it happens, is also the trait which distinguishes them absolutely from all other populations. Language.

It would be nice to know exactly when language became a human characteristic. The physical capacity to speak must have been a product of genetic variation; but when did it arise? Was speech the talent which made the handaxe toolmakers so successful? Or did it arrive with modern humans? Was the spectacular proliferation of skills and cultural behaviour which began 50,000 years ago the result of improved communication between individuals? Did the Neanderthals disappear because they lacked the communicative skills of the newly arrived modern humans?

The fossil evidence offers few answers. Almost nothing of the vocal tract is preserved, and reconstructions have inspired more controversy than incontrovertible answers. Some experts have said that the australopithecines were no more able to speak than a modern chimpanzee, while the Neanderthals had only a limited capacity for speech. Others argue that braincasts taken from fossil skull interiors show bumps and fissures in the cerebral cortex which indicate a limited capacity for speech in the australopithecines, and a full ability to talk in the Neanderthals. Such divergent conclusions must throw doubt on the validity of even attempting to answer the question on the basis of the available evidence. And as to whether or not early man possessed the physical ability to talk, a cynic has pointed out that even a parrot could discuss the merits of the argument if a human brain could be connected to the equipment which enables the bird to say 'pretty Polly'. In other words, software matters most, not hardware.

But no one doubts that the capacity to speak and thus pass information between individuals, among groups and from generation to generation was the supreme talent which our ancestors acquired on their long evolutionary journey. Speech was the ultimate innovation. Whenever it arose, it must have been a crucial aspect of the new skills and lifestyles which began to proliferate about 50,000 years ago, and certainly must have accelerated the trends which enabled mankind to multiply and occupy virtually every ecological niche which the world has to offer.

The consensus of informed opinion is that speech probably developed with the advent of modern man, populations of whom were dispersed throughout Africa well before 100,000 years ago, and the comparative analysis of spoken languages has proved immensely useful in reconstructing those portions of African history which both science and the written word have left unrecorded; this has been especially true in respect of the dispersal of pastoral and agricultural people, such as the Maasai and the Kikuyu.

The comparative analysis of language is a complex affair, though its basic assumptions are simple enough. All the languages of the world can be grouped into a number of distinct families, and the languages within each family are related (to varying degrees) by common features of vocabulary, grammar and pronunciation. By analysing the prevalence of these common features, linguists are able to draw some conclusions as to how long the various languages have been developing separately. A standard list of the words used to describe basic entities and activities (such as sun, people, water, drinking and so on) provides a primary measure. Clearly, the languages with the highest percentage of words in common will be those which split from the ancestral tongue most recently, and *vice versa*. In addition to this largely statistical analysis, linguists also try to establish the root form of significant (though possibly very different) words in related languages, and to identify 'loanwords' which have been absorbed into one language from another; by these means they can reconstruct hypothetical proto-languages and suggest timetables for the splitting and dispersal of the languages within each group and family.

The African languages fall into four distinct linguistic families: Khoisan, Afroasiatic, Nilo-Saharan and Niger-Congo, and though there has been a good deal of intermingling among them, the distinctive nature of each group remains evident not only in the language, but also in the typical appearance, distribution and lifestyle of the people concerned.

The Khoisan speakers are the light-skinned hunters and gatherers of the Kalahari and south-west Africa (better known as the Hottentots and Bushmen perhaps, though these terms now have a distinctly pejorative connotation), remnants of a once more widespread population which was replaced by or absorbed into the groups now occupying their former territories. The Afroasiatic family is typified by the Somalis and Ethiopians, though it also includes many other people of the Sahara, north Africa and the Near East. The Nilo-Saharan family includes the Maasai of East Africa, and the pastoralists occupying the savannahs which extend from Cameroon across the southern Sudan to Ethiopia, and north into Chad. The fourth family, the Niger-Congo, dominates Africa south of the Sahara. Its distribution extends south of a line drawn from Senegal in the west to Kenya in the east, and is total except for some isolated pockets of other groups in east and central Africa, and the region occupied by the Khoisan in south west Africa. The Bantu farmers constitute the largest part of the Niger-Congo family, and they of course include the Kikuyu who have settled around Mount Kenya.

Linguistic analysis shows that the Maasai and the Kikuyu are not at all closely related, but finds an ancient association with food production in all the African languages (except in the

Khoisan languages, where only a recent association is evident). Reconstructions of the root words for such things as 'cow', 'donkey', 'grain' and 'cultivate' suggest that food production was well established among the Afroasiatic people by 7,000 years ago; and a very widespread distribution of two root words for cattle among the Nilo-Saharan languages implies that they had a no less general and ancient association with pastoralism.

More specifically, the analysis of modern languages in East Africa has led linguists to conclude that waves of cattle-owning people began advancing into the Rift Valley from the southern Sudan and the Ethiopian highlands between 6,000 and 4,000 years ago. Each wave absorbed or displaced the preceding wave, implanting tell-tale clues of association in each other's language. The Maa speakers, the Maasai and the Samburu, were the most recent to arrive, and the evidence suggests that they began herding cattle on the grasslands to the northwest of Mount Kenya at the same time as the Kikuyu began planting crops on the south-eastern slopes of the mountain.

The dispersal of the Bantu-speaking peoples which brought the Kikuyu to Mount Kenya is one of the most remarkable episodes of migration and colonization in world history, though it is not widely known. The process began some 2,300 years ago, among Bantu farmers settled in the well-watered and fertile lands to the west of Lake Victoria, in eastern Zaire, Rwanda, and around the shores of Lake Tanganyika.

It is thought likely that the advent of the iron age in central Africa was the root cause of the dispersal. Forests were easier to clear and the land was easier to cultivate with iron tools; more food was produced, and more people could be supported. Eventually there were too many people. By the beginning of the Christian era, waves of Bantu farmers were advancing steadily away from the great lakes region. By 200 AD they had spread across east Africa to the Indian Ocean; by 600 AD they had moved southward through what is now Tanzania, Malawi and Mozambique to the coast of southern Africa, and westward through southern Zaire and Zambia into Angola. By 1100 AD the transition to iron age farming in sub-equatorial Africa was complete. Virtually every suitable tract of land had been taken over by the Bantu farmers. Pre-existing hunter-gatherers and pastoralists were either absorbed into the new agricultural society, or had become symbiotic elements of a new expanded economy. In many cases they followed their traditional ways of life for centuries after the arrival of the iron age farmers.

Today there are more than 300 Bantu languages, spoken by more than 130 million people. But the Bantu expansion, though remarkably rapid and pervasive, was not absolute. Most of what is now southern Angola, Namibia, Botswana and the Cape Province of South Africa was too dry for the Bantu farmers, and their crops were unsuited to the winter rainfall, Mediterranean-type climate of the well-watered western Cape, just as the Egyptian cereals had been unsuited to the summer rainfall, tropical climate of the Bantu homeland (see page 33). Thus the entire south-western corner of Africa was left untouched by the Bantu farmers, and became the last homeland of the Khoisan-speaking hunter-gatherers and pastoralists, who were neither numerous enough, nor well-armed enough to deter the ambitions of the Europeans who came ashore at Table Bay in the 17th century.

The absence of settled Bantu farmers in the vicinity of Cape Town's natural harbour gave the European settlers a foothold they found nowhere else on the continent: good water, good land, a climate suited to European crops, and no competition. And the consequences reverberate to this day.

But while the south-western corner of the continent lay virtually empty, the Bantu farmers radiated from population centres in the equatorial regions of east and central Africa during the first thousand years of the Christian era. The Kikuyu are one of many groups descended from Bantu populations which moved steadily north-eastward from the vicinity of Lake Tanganyika during the 11th century AD.

As they advanced around the southern shores of Lake Victoria, through the highland of northern Tanzania, via Kilimanjaro, along the rim of the Rift Valley to the welcoming bulk of Mount Kenya, the migrants split and diverged like the branches of a rapidly growing tree. Small groups settled here, joined other farmers there, mingled with pastoralists, and established symbiotic ties with hunters and gatherers; doubtless some groups succumbed to sleeping sickness or malaria. There was conflict too, but the overall momentum of the dispersal was that of expansion rather than conquest; the process spanned a thousand years; it was slow but inexorable.

Such continuous dispersal of expanding groups of farmers led to the creation of numerous closely related but independent populations throughout East Africa. They shared recent common ancestries and followed similar lifestyles, but each soon developed a sense of quite separate identity. Language played a major role in this development. Languages diverge rapidly in isolation, creating myth and distant history in the space of just a few generations, and drawing people together with a shared belief in their own unique origin and destiny.

By the late nineteenth century when Europeans began to define their 'spheres of influence' in East Africa, and applied the word 'tribe' to the different groups of people they encountered, the process of dispersal and divergence had produced nearly 200 distinct ethnic populations among the farmers and pastoralists and surviving hunter-gatherers of the region. Very few had spoken their own language, or existed independently, for more than a few hundred years, but most were quick to see the advantage of claiming unique and extensive antiquity when the newly-arrived administrators introduced the novel idea of traditional land rights.

'Land was not a problem until the colonial powers arrived,' declares Godfrey Muriuki. 'Within each group there was always room for people to move out and settle beyond the present limits of cultivation. The Kikuyu have a catch-phrase, "going to the frontier", which is used even now when someone takes on a challenging task, but it comes originally from the tradition of moving out to clear new land.'

Godfrey Muriuki's book, *A History of the Kikuyu 1500-1900*, sets the jumble of myth and belief surrounding the origin and settlement of people around Mount Kenya firmly in the context of broader knowledge concerning the recent history of East Africa. As a result, the book has itself become a focus of belief in the modern era of national identity and educated enquiry in Kenya.

Muriuki based his account of Kikuyu history largely upon a mass of oral evidence collected in interviews with Kikuyu elders and other knowledgeable informants during 1967. From this evidence he was able to identify named age-sets, and reconstruct a line of descent dating back to 1512 AD, although the earliest of these age-sets were named only in the vaguest of terms: *Tene*, 'long ago'; *Agu*, 'ancestors', and *Manjiri*, 'creation'.

The most distant ancestors of the Kikuyu came from the Nyambene Hills, to the north-east of Mount Kenya, writes Muriuki, whence they advanced steadily on to the eastern and southern foothills of the mountain. The pioneers found a region of good soils, moderate temperatures, unusually adequate rainfall, and totally free of the tsetse and malarial mosquito which restricted human habitation in other parts. But the foothills were not free of people. Groups of hunters and gatherers, now recalled as the Gumba, the Athi, and the Ndorobo, were already in occupation.

The hunters and gatherers were steadily absorbed or displaced as progressive waves of the Kikuyu pioneers moved on to the mountain and pushed back the forest on all fronts. Muriuki quotes an early British administrator's account of the process: 'The Akikuyu pushed on and on. Their progress was like that of the locusts – the ranks at the rear, finding food supply exhausted, taking wing over the backs of the main body to drop to ground in the forefront. And as locusts clear a sturdy crop, so have the Akikuyu cleared the forest.'

As the main body of the Kikuyu pioneers advanced southward through the foothills, small groups broke away, and moved up the ridges to clear forest and found centres of agricultural activity at higher elevations. These groups remained as the ancestors of the tribal groups now known as the Chuka, the Embu, the Mbeere, the Gicugu, and the Ndia – all closely related to the Kikuyu. (The Meru, who occupy the north-eastern foothills of the mountain, were another group of Bantu emigrants who arrived from the coast during the late 1700s.)

From the evidence of oral history, Muriuki has calculated that large numbers of the pioneer Kikuyu settled around Ithanga at the confluence of the Thika and Thagana rivers, about 80km due south of the Mount Kenya peaks, by the beginning of the 17th century. As its population increased, Ithanga became a major centre of dispersal. Some groups returned to reinforce the Embu, Mbeere, Ndia and Gicugu populations on the south-eastern shoulder of the mountain; other groups moved north-west up the tributaries of the Thagana and founded another centre of settlement and dispersal on the slopes of the Nyandarua Range, facing Mount Kenya. This is the place which has become known as the birthplace of the Kikuyu people; they called it Mukurue wa Gathanga, 'the Garden of Eden of Kikuyu traditions', as Muriuki describes it.

Muriuki's evidence indicates that the Kikuyu pioneers established their settlement at the Mukurue wa Gathanga early in the 17th century. The land was fertile, highly suited to intensive agriculture, and of the pioneers who had hitherto retained an element of hunting and pastoralism in their lifestyle, the majority converted to full-time farming. The population increased rapidly, fuelling further waves of dispersal: west into the Nyanduruas, south to the present site of Nairobi, north to the Nyeri plains and the Laikipia Plateau. It was during this period of expansion, as the Kikuyu discovered a formidable talent for intensive agriculture, that their symbiotic relationship with the Maasai was established. Goods were exchanged, words borrowed and customary practices adopted. There was a good deal of inter-marriage too – so much so that many of Muriuki's informants claimed Maasai descent, and more than half the Kikuyu of some districts are believed to have Maasai blood in their veins.

The Kikuyu reached the limits of their expansion during the latter part of the 18th century. After generations of advance, the problems of poor land, territorial conflict with adjacent groups, and harassment by remnants of the Gumba and the Athi, persuaded the pioneers that going to the frontier was no longer the best option. They turned back, and it was this development, writes Muriuki, which led to the emergence of a single self-identifying group of people –

the Kikuyu – from the inherent diversity of the pioneers. It happened no more than 200 years ago. Clans and families which previously would have split and diverged became increasingly inclined to consolidate their interests on one ridge of the mountain slope. The land of the Mukurue wa Gathanga became a precious symbol of Kikuyu unity, and the story of Gikuyu and Mumbi instilled a deep shared belief that the Kikuyu possessed an exclusive God-given right to live there, on the land facing Mount Kenya.

The forest edge on the south-eastern foothills of Mount Kenya. The summit (top right) stands 50km beyond.

Forest path on the Chogoria route to the peaks.

East African redwood (*Hagenia abyssinica*) grows on the massif at elevations
between 2850m and 3000m, often festooned with lichen.

The Chogoria route passes through extensive thickets of mountain bamboo (*Arundinaria alpina*), a giant grass (right) which grows up to 15m in height. Very few plants can live in its shade (above).

Children at Tharene, home village of the Mount Kenya zealot, Efreme M'Kiara.

CHAPTER FIVE

Chogoria

I arrived in Embu country on a Friday afternoon. Two or three hundred years after the Embu themselves. Travelling courtesy of a new road built with British aid; speeding over tarmac where, until 1988, the Embu and any other travellers to the region had bounced uncomfortably over a deteriorating track which wound through the ridges and valleys of the foothills. The shape and soils of the landscape testified to its forest origin, though tea, coffee, maize and pasture had replaced many of the trees.

On a ridge above Chogoria, on the old road beyond the tarmac, Livingstone Barine farms a portion of the land that an astute great-grandfather secured for his descendents a century or so ago by the simple strategy of assisting the British when they assumed administrative control of the region. While his clansmen contested British claims to sovereignty, old man Barine accepted the inevitable. He welcomed and helped the white men. In return he was made a chief, and subsequently became owner of a large parcel of land.

The land has been split and divided among the heirs of each generation since then, but sizeable portions still remain intact. Livingstone has a hectare or two of coffee and tea, a large plantation of bananas, gardens for maize and vegetables, and pasture for cattle and goats. Farming and efficient food production are his passion, he says, but his job teaching physics at the Chogoria Boys' High School does not allow him much opportunity to work on the land. In Africa, a man's inability to farm should not matter, for wives customarily do most of the work in subsistence agriculture. Livingstone's wife, however, is a nurse employed at the Chogoria General Hospital. She too has little time for farming. Consequently, the labour on the Barine holding is provided by a number of relatives who live on the farm. 'We Embu live as extended families,' Livingstone explained as he gestured expansively about the compound to which he had invited me. 'That's my brother's house. Another brother and his wife live there. That's my uncle's ...'

The buildings Livingstone pointed out were built of sawn timber, roofed with corrugated iron. One, in which his father lived, had a small balcony. They were set about the compound more by the influence of need than of design. Certainly, their disposition showed little sign of having been affected by the edicts of any local planning authority. Put a building wherever there was convenient space for it, seemed to have been the policy on the Barine estate. And if the need to accommodate another family arose, construct a house for them somewhere among the others. The result is a collection of buildings and people almost large enough to be called a hamlet. The buildings encircle a sloping patch of grass too steep for building upon, but cropped by goats to the standard of an acceptable lawn. A standpipe rising above a concrete plinth at the foot of the slope provides water for the compound. Women congregate there. Children play on the grass and between the houses. Chickens run free underfoot. A saloon car which probably was capable of taking the road not too long ago, stands between the main house and a hen house, facing pens where the goats are housed at night. Grass grows lank around the wheels. Close by the gate, the trunk of a dying tree supports a splendid straggle of brilliant mauve-flowering bougainvillaea.

Livingstone and his immediate family once occupied one or more of the wooden buildings in the compound, but he now lives in a house of cement-block and brick construction on the lower side of the compound. The house faces east; at night, the moon shines into the bedrooms, but the rising sun is hidden by the surrounding trees and by the early morning mists which frequently rise from the valleys.

The house is not quite finished, Livingstone explained, lacking ceiling boards in some rooms, and final plastering in others. One also sensed that an entrepreneurial talent had directed its construction thus far. Rooms had been planned and built as the funds for materials and labour became available; and would be completed by a similar process. Electricity would be connected soon; the telephone was already installed. Running water was constantly available, and came from the same source that supplied the standpipe in the compound – a tank constructed by Livingstone on a stream 10kms up the mountain slope, from which he laid a pipe to his property. 'Purest water in the world. Much better than you drink at home,' he declared.

Livingstone lived in London for a time during the three years he spent abroad as a student and was not impressed. He found Londoners unfriendly and their living conditions depressing. He was indifferent to the British weather, which is an unusual reaction, but said he found Britain itself to be all the British people deserve – leaving one to wonder if he meant that the British were not worthy of anything better.

Mercurial is an adjective that might be applied to Livingstone Barine, but it is not one that would come to mind at first sight. He is middle-aged, of medium height, and a little on the stout side. Jackets pull tight around his waist, and he looks as though he would be more comfortable in an armchair than moving about as energetically as he does. But conversation soon corrects the sedentary impression. Like many teachers, he is more inclined to offer monologues than to indulge in dialogue; and while dialogue can be conducted from the depths of armchairs, a teacher's monologues are usually rattled off while pacing about and gesticulating before a silent and captive audience. So it is with Livingstone Barine. The volume and tone of voice vary with the speed of delivery, jokes slot in neatly as perfectly grammatical sub-clauses. He pauses for the laugh, then moves on to the next carefully formulated point. And the movement is physical as well as conversational. Livingstone Barine is an energetic, as well as an intelligent man; he is also something of an innovator.

'You want to see my biogas plant,' he said, heading briskly towards the coffee plantation before I could decide whether his statement was a question or an instruction. 'We cook by gas,' he added. 'Completely self-sufficient system. You must see it.'

Passing through the coffee, we mounted the slope beyond the compound and emerged on a ridge where a cattle stall had been constructed. Four Jersey cows with well-filled udders were munching contentedly at quantities of fresh green fodder. The concrete floor of the stall sloped towards a central channel in which the cows' manure collected when the floor was washed down each evening. From the channel, the effluent flowed down a pipe into a circular concrete pond.

'That's the digester, where bacteria convert the manure to methane gas,' Livingstone explained as we scrambled down the slope and stood beside the pond of effluent. 'And that's our gas storage tank,' he added, pointing proudly to a dome of roughly welded, black-painted steel – about one-and-a-half metres in diameter – that rose like some misplaced conning tower from the turgid contents of the pond.

'The tank rises as gas is produced, and falls as we use it. The tank was made to my specifications by a welder down in Chogoria. It weighs several hundred kilos, but it floats on the gas,' he told me in the tones of amazed revelation that children are accustomed to hearing from enthusiastic teachers. I wondered aloud if there was a danger of the tank exploding under pressure, smothering the compound in effluent, and gassing its occupants. He dismissed my frivolity with the precise tones he might have used on an impertinent pupil. 'The system is fitted with a safety valve,' he said, and turned from the digester and tank to the slope below.

'Now this is where my circle of self-sufficiency is made complete,' he said as we stood on a broad ledge carved into the slope beneath the digester. Before us was a rectangular pond of swimming pool proportions, filled to the brim with water the colour and consistency of a light chocolate milkshake. 'My fishpond,' Livingstone said, taking a pace backward and making a introductory gesture with the right hand. And indeed, the movement of many fish was discernible on the surface, though the water was too cloudy to see more than a few millimetres into it.

Livingstone resumed his schoolmasterly demeanour. 'When the digester pond becomes too full, effluent overflows and runs down the slope towards the fish pond,' he explained. 'Here on the level ground it collects in puddles; algae grow on the surface – you can see it there, bright green – every day or so we sweep the algae into the pond, and the fish feed on it. Tilapia and carp.'

'But do the fish grow well in such murky waters?' I ventured to ask, 'and how do they taste?'

'Ideal conditions, ideal conditions,' he replied, 'warm water, plenty of sunlight, plenty of food, the fish thrive.' Ignoring the question of taste, he summarized the benefits of his remarkable installation.

'The cows feed on grass and produce milk for us; bacteria feed on the manure and produce gas for us, algae feed on the surplus manure, the fish feed on the algae, and we feed on the fish. It's a completely self-sufficient system. Every household should have one. Many people have been to see it. They are amazed. The British High Commissioner came to see it, and he was amazed.'

The tour of the biogas installation had taken all of ten minutes. Now Livingstone turned and walked briskly back towards the compound. 'My wife will have made tea for us,' he said. 'We will drink that, then I will take you to meet Efreme, the man who climbs Mount Kenya in ordinary clothes and without shoes – yes! all the way to the top. But first you must see another invention: my high-speed pyrethrum dryer.'

Pyrethrum, a perennial herb from which the natural insecticide is produced, is an important crop on high-altitude farms in Kenya. The toxic element is contained in the flowers; drying the flowers for packing and transportation is a tedious and time-consuming procedure. 'It can take days, even when the weather is fine,' Livingstone declared. 'The flowers have to be spread out in the open, turned as they dry, brought inside if it rains — my dryer solves all those problems.'

The dryer had been displayed at the Agricultural Show in Nairobi not long before, and was not yet completely reassembled following its journey back to Chogoria. Its two main components occupied the greater part of Livingstone's verandah. The first was a very large rectangular box covered with a sheet of glass and enclosing pieces of sheet metal ingeniously arranged to create a long and labyrinthine air-passage between slots at either end of the box. When the box was erected at an angle of about 45 degrees in the open, the metal was warmed through the glass; air drawn in by convection at the bottom slot was heated as it passed over the metal, and emerged as a veritable blast of hot air from the slot at the top. From the slot, the hot air was conducted to the operative part of the dryer: a large cupboard fitted with slatted shelves on which the pyrethrum was spread for drying.

'This will dry a crop in a matter of hours, instead of days,' declared Livingstone, giving his invention a hearty slap.

'It was working at the Show, and people were very impressed. The British High Commissioner came to see it, and he said it should be made available in kit form. I am looking into that.'

On entering the house from the verandah, Livingstone found that his wife, though returned from the hospital, had not yet made tea. 'Never mind, we will go without,' he said. 'Let us now go to see the zealot, Efreme,' and passing through the house without pause we left by the front door and took to the car.

Efreme lives in a village near Meru called Tharene. Hastening in that direction along the new road linking Embu and Meru, Livingstone declared that, with this road, the British had also brought an element of population control to the region.

'Scores of people are dying on this road. See that,' he said, pointing to a smashed safety fence at the apex of a curve, 'a bus went through there. Many people died. And there,' indicating a corner on which workmen were re-erecting another stretch of battered fence. In less than 20 km, we passed numerous places at which vehicles had left the road in the previous four weeks with destructive, though not always fatal results. Gangs of men working on the safety fences were hard-pressed to keep up with the damage.

The new road winds through the undulating foothills of Mount Kenya. It is built to high specifications; the curves are perfectly engineered to maintain maximum speed. 'Trouble is,' Livingstone declared, 'drivers here are very good on bad roads, and very bad on good roads. They can get a car through mud and dust, but they don't know how to handle a car at speed on a tarmac road. So they kill themselves. There is a selection process at work,' he continued, pursuing a train of thought attractive to any science teacher. 'Bad drivers are killed, good drivers survive. Eventually, there will be only good drivers and our roads will be safe. But how long will the process take? That should be an examination question. Answer on one side of the paper only.'

Tharene consists of a football pitch (without goalposts) surrounded by blocks of dukas (shops). The dukas were barred and bolted when we arrived, and none of the men lounging about the perimeter of the field knew for certain where Efreme might be found. Livingstone hurried off towards the cultivated land beyond the village where it was thought he might still be working. As the light faded, and children gathered to giggle at the incongruity of my presence, and laugh at the inadequacy of my Kiswahili, a tall, very thin man appeared from behind the dukas and weaved his way across the field towards me. At first I thought he was staggering through the last appalling stages of AIDS, but as he drew closer I realised that he was merely suffering from an excess of alcohol. Indeed, as I stood to greet him, I was even able to identify the drink itself – there was more than a taint of maize beer on his breath.

'I am the sub-chief for this location,' he announced with as much authority as his condition allowed, 'why are you here?' As I described the reason for my visit, he impatiently jingled a large bunch of keys hanging from his belt. 'You cannot come here and interview people without permission,' he said when I had finished. 'You must have permission before you come.' I explained that what I intended was not so much an interview with Efreme, as a conversation,

Waiting for Efreme M'Kiara at Tharene.

and asked if there was a law forbidding visitors to meet and converse with Kenyans. He ignored the question and began to talk about national security and fears that spies were roaming the country. 'You must have a permit to come here,' he said again, clearly implying that without a permit I was likely to be suspected of spying.

Meanwhile, a crowd of villagers and children had gathered around us, from amongst whom Livingstone emerged some minutes later, bringing with him the slight figure of a man in cord trousers and bare feet: Efreme. Livingstone asked what was going on, then used his teaching talents to masterly effect. He addressed the sub-chief in English: 'This man is a visitor from England,' he began. 'One day, your children may visit his country. What will you think of England if they come back and tell you they were greeted there as you have greeted this man today?' The sub-chief replied in the vernacular, at some length. Livingstone told him it was impolite to use a language a guest could not understand, and asked him to speak English. The sub-chief said I needed a permit. I took from my pocket a letter from Perez Olindo, the Director of Kenya National Parks, and asked if that would do. The letter welcomed my plans to write a book on Mount Kenya, and seemed to satisfy the sub-chief. He read it aloud to the crowd (by then quite large), and they expressed general approval. Then attention turned to Efreme.

Efreme M'Kiara achieved national fame in 1979, when a group of climbers found him sitting on the top of Nelion, barefoot and dressed only in ragged street clothes. Ascending Nelion is a difficult and demanding climb, there is no easy route. The summit is 5188m above sea level, open to the elements and extremely cold. Given the facts of the encounter, the climbers assumed that Efreme had accompanied another party up the peak, and was taking care of their belongings while they tackled the adjacent peak, Batian. But this hardly explained his appearance, and there were no other belongings. When they spoke to him and offered help, Efreme scurried away. Eventually, the time came for the climbers to begin their descent, and they were obliged to leave the mystery unresolved. Later, from the base of the peak, they saw Efreme making his descent. They watched in awe as he scrambled down rockfaces without the benefit of ropes or companionable assistance, barefoot and inadequately dressed in conditions that test even the most experienced rock climbers.

When this encounter on the summit of Nelion was reported in the Kenya press, it became known that this was not the first time that Efreme had climbed the mountain. Rangers reported that he had been seen in the vicinity on a number of occasions. All of Mount Kenya above 10,000 feet (about 3000m) has been designated a national park, and initially the rangers were anxious only to ensure that Efreme had paid his entrance fee, but as repeated encounters made it clear that he was determined to reach the summit itself, they became concerned for his safety as well. He was seen at high elevations on the mountain, but ran away whenever challenged. Something of a competition developed between the Efreme and the rangers – he trying to climb the mountain, they trying to stop him.

That he succeeded there is no doubt, though how often is not known. That he was able to scale the peak can only be due to his personal attributes – exceptional tolerance of cold and of oxygen deprivation, remarkable physical strength and unswerving determination.

The rangers, with first-hand experience of the severe conditions frequently encountered on Mount Kenya, were inclined to regard Efreme as a madman, or, at the very least, as one possessed. Too many ill-prepared people are injured or die on the mountain for them to regard his behaviour as that of a fully rational being. Further afield, however, in the more comfortable environments where newspaper articles are written and read, Efreme's determination to sit on the top of Mount Kenya, alone, whenever he chose, was seen as an expression of deep religious conviction. Mount Kenya is the spiritual heart of the nation, many believed. Efreme climbed the peak to pray, and to be close to god, they said. In the popular image, he was a zealot, fulfilling ambitions that every Kenyan should recognize.

Efreme, confronted in the ring of villagers at Tharene, had the stature of a child. He was no larger than the twelve- and thirteen-year-olds standing behind him. Narrow shoulders, slight chest, slim hips, thin limbs – height about 1.5 metres; weight 40kgs, perhaps. I felt that I could have grasped him about the waist and lifted him above my head, as one might deal with a playful child. But there was nothing playful about Efreme. His legs, feet and toes curled inward, so that he stood more on the edges than on the soles of his feet. His hair hung in dreadlocks; the lines of his face stretched taut from the turned-down corners of his mouth, tightly shut. The chin was raised slightly, drawing out the loose skin of an old man's neck; the eyes were elusive, responding neither to a smile nor a spoken greeting. He shook his head before responding to Livingstone's opening remarks. Efreme cannot speak English, so the conversation was conducted in the Meru language.

Livingstone translated. 'I have told Efreme that you have come from England to write about Mount Kenya and that you would like to hear about his experiences on the mountain,' he said. 'He says that he cannot talk to you now. You must write a letter asking for an appointment to come and see him another time.' The sub-chief nodded vigorously.

Though there was little hope of my being able to return to Tharene I said, yes, I would write first. As we said goodbye, I offered Efreme some money. He shied away from it, shaking his head as though trying to dislodge some awful idea. Livingstone told me to give the money to some children, whom he instructed to pass it on to Efreme. The children gathered around him, poking the notes at him, laughing, while Efreme, still shaking his head, wrapped his arms around his body and danced about, avoiding their attempts to push the money in his jacket pockets like a taunted bear. It was an appalling sight, and makes a sad memory to have brought away from Tharene, but Livingstone dismissed my concern for Efreme.

Livingstone did not share the reverence for Efreme and his feats that I had encountered in Nairobi; nor did most other people who actually knew the man, he said. According to Livingstone, Efreme was the deluded victim of his experiences as a freedom fighter, when he had joined the bands of men waging their war of independence from the depths of the forests on Mount Kenya. Efreme remained in the forest even after independence had been won, and by the time he left he was incapable of merging painlessly back into society.

'So he has turned himself into a one-man religion,' Livingstone concluded with a dismissive laugh. But no one who has followed Efreme's route up Mount Kenya can dismiss his achievement quite so readily.

Back at Chogoria, Livingstone introduced me to Lloyfor Mutegi, the man he had asked to act as my guide on the mountain. Lloyfor is an experienced guide whose quiet-spoken and assured manner inspires immediate confidence. Unfolding my large-scale survey map of the mountain, I explained that I wanted to spend a few nights camped at Lake Alice, which lies at about 3500m on the moorland well to the east of the track which leads to the main peaks. I pointed to the lake on the map – an indistinct blob in a tangle of contours marking the steepness and irregularity of the terrain. When asked, Lloyfor said he had been there; the lake was about two hours from the roadhead, he added. This surprised me. At the Mountain Club I had been told that very few people know that part of the mountain. A member who had led an expedition to Lake Alice in 1986 had shown me the route his party had taken through the unmarked terrain; the lake is about four hours from the roadhead, he had said.

'Not Lake Ellis,' I said to Lloyfor, suspecting some confusion with a better-known lake less than two hours north of the roadhead, 'Lake Alice. Lake a - liss. Not Lake e - liss.'

'Yes, I know it. Lake ay – liss. I have been there,' Lloyfor repeated with calm authority.

Livingstone's wife served bowls of maize, and rice, and beans, and a meat stew for supper. We drank tea after eating, and talked to his 86-year-old father, George Barine, about Embu life earlier in the century. It has never been easy, he said. All the work was done by hand – there were no ploughs, no draught animals, and the limitations of manual labour on difficult terrain denied people the chance of producing food for more than their immediate needs. There was hardly ever a surplus that they could store for later use. Consequently, when the rains failed, people had to call for the help of clansmen living in other regions, or move to new land. There was always plenty of new land available in those days, he said, but not now.

I asked about the mountain. People were afraid of the place, he replied. Not until the white men arrived did anyone think of going there. The mountain was just a remote part of the landscape where the sun went down. When things were going well it was hardly thought of, but in times of calamity it was provident to regard the peak as a place where God resided, since he clearly did not reside among people. In bad times, the people made sacrifices facing the mountain, praying for help. They did not know that the whiteness on the mountain was snow and ice. How could they have known? They knew nothing of snow and ice and assumed the whiteness was white rock.

When we retired for the night, Livingstone escorted me by the light of a candle to the room where I would sleep. He set the candle and its saucer carefully on the floor and slapped the box that I had assumed was to serve as my bedside table. 'What do you think this is?' he asked. The box, virtually a cube in its proportions, stoutly-made with dovetail joints and a well-fitting lid, clearly was intended to be more than a bedside table, but I could only think of a linen chest. 'No, and you would never guess,' Livingstone replied. 'It's another of my inventions. A solar oven.' He removed the lid and showed me the cooking trays and heat-traps within. 'These arrangements will concentrate solar energy to produce temperatures in excess of 200 degrees centigrade, even when the sky is overcast,' he said. 'The oven will cook meat, bread, soups. But I still have to get the mirror made ... I am working on that.'

Tea plantation and smallholdings on the foothills above Chogoria.

Hives placed high in the forest provide honey for Embu smallholders.

CHAPTER SIX

Urumandi

The eastern valleys and ridges of Mount Kenya are tucked into the mountain like folds around the edge of a ruckled pillow. The steeply rising and falling slopes are the product of ancient volcanic upheaval and erosion. Congenial climatic conditions have since covered them with dense forest and, over the millennia, the natural cycles of forest growth and decay have created a deep layer of soil which smoothed out the irregularities of ridgetop and valley alike. Now that most of the trees have been removed from the lower slopes, and replaced by agricultural crops, plantations and pasture, the smooth undulations produced in this way are particularly striking. The sweep of a coombe, the slope of a ridge, the curve of a valley – in all these aspects, the contours of the land seem precisely designed and engineered. As indeed they were, by the Earth's own creative processes. The landscape is beautiful – not least because there is no sign of the abuse that mars the exploitation of forest land in other parts. Fact is, the Embu practise utilization rather than exploitation. Their farming is longterm and, after a century or two of subsistence agriculture on the slopes of Mount Kenya, it is perhaps not surprising that their methods defer to the constraints of the environment. Substantial numbers of forest trees remain standing; permanent tea and coffee plantations hold the ground as effectively as the trees they replace; cultivated slopes are terraced.

Lloyfor Mutegi lives some distance to the west of Chogoria on a piece of land that curves sharply around the head of a narrow valley. The house, made of wood, stands on a ledge cut into the steep slope; bananas, citrus trees and passion-fruit vines grow in its immediate vicinity; potatoes and other vegetables grow just beyond, and rows of coffee and tea are ranged around the steep slopes of the coombe below like rows of seats in an amphitheatre. From the house at the top of the coombe, Lloyfor and his family have a splendid uninterrupted view down the valley to the village and the school the children attend from the age of six. The school is 5km away, and the children walk there and back each day.

Lloyfor has three cows, which graze on pasture at the top of the ridge, but he has no biogas plant below their stall. His wife fetches water from a spring in the valley, and he sees little prospect of finding the money to pipe it to the house. Nor does he envisage connection to the electricity supply. His land and his income are both a good deal smaller than Livingstone's.

When ownership of the Embu lands was ajudicated, the Mutegi family was given title to a large holding. 'But my father made mistakes and had to sell land,' Lloyfor explained. His father managed to find money for the secondary and higher education of Lloyfor's older brothers, but there was none for Lloyfor himself.

The brothers secured good jobs in the civil service after leaving school, and have settled in Nairobi, but Lloyfor has been obliged to live off what remains of the family holding. It is large enough to provide food for the family, but not large enough to grow cash crops such as coffee and tea in quantities that will buy household essentials and pay for the children's schooling.

So Lloyfor supplements his income with work as a mountain guide, but the amounts involved are not substantial. His daily fee would not pay for the train ticket that a commuter from Windsor to London must buy each day, for example. Moreover, the impracticability of climbing the mountain during the rains means that Lloyfor can expect little or no income at all for up to six months of the year: most climbing is done during the three months around August, or the three months around the end of the year. Furthermore, the Chogoria route does not attract large numbers of visitors. Lloyfor might expect to lead just one or two parties on to the mountain each month – 10 or 12 days work in all.

The Chogoria route does not attract many climbers for the very reasons that those who do use it find most appealing: the route is long and its facilities are minimal. The hike from Chogoria to the peaks takes at least three days; with another day for climbing and two more for the descent, this means a round trip of six days – which is difficult for independent travellers to arrange themselves, and very expensive if arranged by a safari company. Accordingly, most visitors climb the mountain from the west, with one of the safari companies which regularly shunt packaged groups up and down the mountain, via the Naro Moru and Sirimon tracks. By this means it is possible to 'do' Mount Kenya quite economically in a couple of days.

Possible, but hardly desirable, or even advisable. Visitors signing up for such a trip are driven to the roadhead at about 3000m, from whence they must ascend 1200m to their overnight accommodation. Next morning, they may scramble up the remaining 600m or so to the summit of Lenana (4985m, and the only one of Mount Kenya's three main peaks which offers a non-technical ascent) and will descend to the roadhead in the afternoon. Such a schedule – even if extended by a day or two – leaves little time for a visitor to become acclimatized to the altitude and exertion. The idea, I am told, is that altitude has no time to affect the body if the climber climbs and descends in a short space of time. That might work for some highly motivated and exceptionally fit individuals, but for most of humanity it is nonsense.

Lack of oxygen affects everyone who ascends above 3000m, and severely affects those who attempt to hurry. Extreme weariness, headaches and nausea are the symptoms – and acclimatization is the only cure. Even quite unfit climbers will enjoy, rather than endure the experience if they have had time to acclimatize. Three days is usually sufficient. Gradual ascent is the secret, and its benefits are greatly enhanced if climbers can spend some time each day above the altitude at which they will sleep. Ideally, they should set up the overnight camp, then explore the slopes above strenuously before descending for supper and sleep. This strategy encourages a restful night and makes the morning's ascent less daunting.

On the Chogoria route, distance makes gradual ascent and a period of acclimatization unavoidable. But the route has additional attractions. The greater part of the Mount Kenya massif lies on the Chogoria side, east and south east of the peaks. Above the forest, the heather and sugar-bush moorlands rise, ridge upon ridge, 25km to the shale plateaux, the moraines, and the peaks. Early morning, late afternoon, through the changing patterns of sunshine and cloud shadow, the entire mountain is visible on the route from Chogoria, its ascending planes of ridge and valley surmounted by a dog-toothed line of sharp bare rock and snow. And the mountain rises so high above where one instinctively feels the horizon ought to be. Even from the forest edge, the head must be raised several degrees before the eyes look directly at the peaks. The peaks themselves look tiny, the snowfields minuscule, but their erect proportions are fully appropriate to the bulk of the huge mountain they crown: you can already sense how much they will dominate events as the innocent ambition to ascend the intervening elevations becomes arduous reality. By contrast, the shorter western ascents are dominated by a steeply rising foreground; the peaks remain hidden until far into the climb – and then their grandeur eliminates all appreciation of them as part of an even grander whole.

Black-barked camphor trees, rising to 45m in height, dominate the middle
elevations of the Chogoria forest.

Mixed vegetation at the edge of a forest glade, near Riki corner.

The forest is another attraction of the Chogoria route. It is far more dense, more varied and more extensive than the forest on the western side of the mountain. The reason is simply that more rain falls in the east and south. The two seasonal monsoons which bring the greater part of Kenya's rainfall blow in from the south-east during the first half of the year, and from the north-east during the second half (the direction changes as the sun swings across the equator). Striking the mountain from the east, both monsoons bring a preponderance of rain to the eastern side of the mountain, and it is no accident that the forest is most dense and agriculture most dependable in the south-eastern quadrant, where the Embu have settled: the south-east monsoon brings the most rain.

When Lloyfor first accompanied a party of climbers on to the mountain, in 1972, he was engaged as a porter and carried a load of about 20kg. The trail entered the forest above Chogoria at about 2000m and emerged about 24 hours later in the Urumandi glade, at just over 3000m. The distance covered was about 25km; parties customarily stopped for a picnic lunch at the stream by Riki corner, and spent a night camped in the Bairuni glade, a natural clearing at about 2700m. There can be no better way of becoming acclimatized to altitude. The ascent is very gradual indeed, and the forest hides the mountain itself, thus screening the visitor from any demoralizing view of the climb ahead – an important consideration on the first day out. Furthermore, the forest is magnificent, and capable of distracting even the least confident climbers from contemplation of their personal inadequacies.

Few environments can match a tropical forest for the appreciation of life's fecundity that it evokes. Trees, shrubs, vines, creepers, orchids, ferns, fungi, mosses, lichens – all plant forms abound. Mature trees, saplings and fallen giants – all stages of growth and decay are present, often growing one from another. The forest may be surprisingly silent, but a network of paths testifies to the presence of animals that feed on its vegetation – elephant, buffalo, rhinoceros, antelope. Stand still and quiet for a while, joining the silence rather than breaking it, and monkeys will chatter; the cough of a leopard will raise the pulse rate, and the iridescent red of Hartlaub's turaco may flash through a patch of sunlight.

The vegetation is always profuse, but its character varies with changing conditions. This is true of all environments, of course, but it is especially true of tropical forests on elevated places like Mount Kenya, where the dominant species of tree, for example, changes completely with every few 100m of altitude. The changing character of the forest is particularly evident on the Chogoria route, and a relaxed ascent makes it gratifyingly apparent to even the most unpractised eye.

The lower levels of the Chogoria forest are distinguished by the tall white bare trunks of the mutati (*Polyscias kikuyuensis*), and the spinach-green leaves of the Meru oak (*Vitex keniensis*); next in elevation comes the zone of the giant camphor (*Ocotea usambarensis*), massive, rough black-barked trees rising 45m from the forest floor; then comes the yellow-wood zone (*Podocarpus milanjianus*), slim, coniferous trees which thrive in the lower temperatures that exclude the camphor and oak from that elevation; the next zone comprises vast stands of bamboo – not a tree, or even a shrub – but a grass growing 12-15m high, and so dense that hardly anything else grows in its midst. The bamboo flowers but once every 100 years, when entire stands will flower simultaneously. Until then, it reproduces vegetatively, and flourishes, but every stem dies after flowering. Then other vegetation takes over – wych hazel, cedar, and a profusion of ground-cover plants while fresh bamboo stands are established elsewhere.

63

The forest landscape opens abruptly above the bamboo zone, presenting a vista of thick grassland, laced with brooks and studded with rocky outcrops around which magnificent specimens of East African rosewood (*Hagenia abyssinica*) grow – massive trees, with broad trunks and a spreading umbrella-shaped crown. The rosewood grows only in the 2850m to 3000m zone. Above that, heathland gradually takes over, to be succeeded in turn by moorland, alpine grassland and finally, the nival zone, where only lichens, some everlastings and a *senecio* capable of withstanding freezing temperatures are able to survive.

If the tropical montane forest above Chogoria is capable of evoking enthusiastic appreciation in visiting climbers, you may be sure that it has long since attracted the attention of people who look at trees with a more acquisitive eye – timber merchants. And indeed, ever since sawmills were brought to the region early this century, Meru oak, camphor, podo, cedar, and East African rosewood have been the raw material of a thriving timber industry, supplying both local and export demands. Camphor, a resilient hardwood ideally suited to truck body construction, was particularly prized; even bamboo was cut for commerce.

That the forest is still so full of impressively large trees is firstly an indication of just how many there were to begin with, and secondly, a credit to the government Forestry Department. All major tracts of forest in Kenya are national reserves; felling is by licence only, and should not exceed rates of regeneration. There have been lamentable lapses in these controls, but some good news too: since the 1970s, the Forestry Department has stipulated that no more living camphor trees may be felled; only dead trees and fallen branches can be taken from the forest. The demand for camphor has since become acute.

As though anticipating the decline of the timber industry, and recognizing a need for alternative enterprise, in 1975 the Meru County Council renovated the forestry road above Chogoria, and extended it to the Urumandi glade, where they built a self-service tourist lodge. It is a rough road, best negotiated by four-wheel-drive vehicles, but it does permit visitors to drive all the way up to 3000m, where they may enjoy some walking and a splendid view from their comfortable rooms – the lodge is very popular. And, of course, the road allows people like me to drive up there too. Shameful, when the forest has so much to offer, but I salved my conscience with a decision to stop and explore the forest on the drive up.

In fact, driving through the forest makes the transition from one vegetation zone to another particularly apparent. The dominant features change swiftly from the vivid green of Meru oak where the sun shines through the leaves, to the rough black trunks of camphor, the thin, dark-green shining leaves of podo, the stands of bamboo, and finally, the rosewood and heath of the moorland at Urumandi glade.

Lloyfor called for the first halt at the corner he called Riki. He said the climbers' trail through the forest was close to the road at that point. A massive camphor tree stood on the corner, indeed, it *was* the corner, the roadmakers clearly having been obliged to make a sharp deviation to avoid it. The trunk was irregular, but at least two metres in diameter; at head-height it divided into three branches, each of considerable dimensions, which spread broadly over the road and the forest behind. Two neatly hewn, hollow cylinders of wood, about one metre long and 40cm wide, stood propped against the trunk. For honey, Lloyfor explained, lifting one to demonstrate how the hives would be hauled high into the tree.

We entered the forest behind the camphor. Within minutes I felt as though we were at the heart of it, and soon began to appreciate how easily one could become lost in such an environ-

Lloyfor, beehives and the massive camphor tree at Riki corner.

ment. There was no point of reference. It was impossible to maintain a sense of direction and orientation as we weaved through the tangle of vegetation. I followed Lloyfor. Vines, saplings, shrubs and ferns blocked the path; mosses and leaf-mould softened our footfall. We climbed over the trunks and branches of fallen giants. At one point, Lloyfor silently signalled a halt and threw a stick at a large rotting branch which lay across the track two or three metres ahead of us. A long black snake slithered away as the stick struck the branch. Lloyfor identified the snake before I could ask. 'Mamba,' he said.

At the edge of a small clearing, where the sun was reflected with surprising, even dazzling, intensity from the shiny leaves of shoulder-high saplings, Lloyfor pointed up into the high canopy beyond. 'Beehive,' he said. I scanned the area he had indicated for some time before distinguishing the solid shape among the shadows of the upper canopy. It was a good 20m up. I wondered how the honey-gatherers managed to find the hives they concealed so well, but then reasoned that if Lloyfor could find them, their owners most certainly could. But what about the bees, why should they use the hive? The forest could hardly be short of natural alternatives. The honey-gatherer attracts the bees to his hives by burning honeycomb in them before putting them in the tree, Lloyfor explained. The smoke drifts widely through the forest, and the scent of honeycomb attracts bees to the hive.

Beyond the clearing, along an incline, we struck the climbers' trail. It was surprisingly broad and unimpeded, considering that climbers had not been using it for some years. 'But it is still used by the animals,' Lloyfor explained. 'Buffalo, elephants and rhinos keep it open,' he said. 'Especially elephants.' And indeed, not far down the trail we encountered the damp droppings, of cannonball proportions, that indicate the recent presence of elephants. 'They passed this way in the night,' Lloyfor explained.

'What do you do if they come this way again?' I asked, able to imagine all too vividly the prospect of meeting an elephant along the trail.

'I am not afraid of that,' he replied.

'Why not?'

'Because I am brave enough. Elephants, even buffalo, cannot make me afraid. If I see them I make a noise – I clap my hands. Then they *must* go away,' he said, putting the stress on an ungrammatical but reassuring imperative.

We met no elephants, nor buffalo. Not even in the bamboo at a higher elevation, where droppings littered a trail wide enough to accommodate two – if not three – elephants abreast. The bamboo, thick as a man's arm and surely up to 12m tall, leaned in over the trail like the roof of a cathedral nave, giving the place an ecclesiastical air. It deserved an altar, or some such point of focus, I thought, upon which the eye might concentrate as the mind absorbed the wonderful improbability of it: a forest of grass. The stems, satin-smooth, green, yellow and golden, teased the eye as you peered away from the trail. They were so straight and regular, so densely packed, that all sense of perspective was lost; vision seemed two-dimensional, and for a moment, I could imagine how touch, smell and sound might be more secure than sight in such a place. The smell of warm earth, the sound of a breeze lightly rustling the topmost leaves of the bamboo, the rattle of heavy stems swaying one against another.

Mountain bamboo on the Chogoria trail.

East African redwoods
(*Hagenia abyssinica*)
and Urumandi glade.

Waterfalls and bathing pools on the Nithi river at Urumandi.

CHAPTER SEVEN

Lake Alice

I spent two nights camped at Urumandi. Acclimatizing. And eating. I walked about among the rosewoods and the streams – it is magnificent hiking country, just as I had been told – but the days were most definitely structured around meals; the preparation and consumption of tasty, nourishing food was my primary interest. I make no bones about it.

When I climbed Kilimanjaro some years before, I had carried enough packets of freeze-dried food to feed a small army, and had eaten hardly any of it. The preparations were commendably light and easy to pack, but that was about all you could say for them, in my opinion. Experimenting beforehand at home, I had been able to disguise the artificial flavour and consume the concoctions, but at altitude, where one eats more from necessity than from appetite, I retched on the stuff. I was determined not to repeat the experience on Mount Kenya (though I did carry an emergency pack of freeze-dried foods), and since I would be travelling without porters much of the time, and therefore unable to carry enough fresh food for all occasions, I took the precaution of eating as much as I could, whenever I could. Eggs and bacon for breakfast; cold meats, cheese and salad for lunch; a wonderful veal stew for supper. Fruit, and large hunks of carrot cake between times; coffee, tea, and lots of drinking chocolate – my stay at Urumandi verged on the orgiastic.

Urumandi Glade was initially put on the map, so to speak, by Ernest Carr, an enthusiast who opened up the Chogoria route in the 1920s. Carr built a hut at the edge of the forest, which remained the overnight stop for parties on the route for many years, falling into disuse only with the construction of the road and the tourist lodge by the Meru County Council. In 1929, Carr loaned the hut to Vivienne de Watteville, a youthful lady who recounts her adventures on the mountain in a book entitled *Speak to the Earth*.

Miss de Watteville lived on the mountain for two months, alone (but for two African servants, whose presence was not reckoned to count as companionship in those days). Her book sparkles with the enthusiasm of an attractive person enjoying novel experiences. I thought of her while following the chain of pools in the river below Nithi Falls, and found myself wondering if she had been altogether unaware of the eroticism which pervades her account of gambolling from pool to pool in that place, naked.

Trout have been introduced to the gin-clear waters of the Nithi since Miss de Watteville's day. Brown trout, quivering as they hold their positions in the fast-flowing stream. Turning, the fish display their beautiful red-splashed sides and remind one immediately of how ubiquitous the dull, profitably-farmed rainbow trout has become. Brown trout were introduced to the Mount Kenya streams in the 1930s by members of that band of men who took trout fry with them to every part of the world where they might thrive, with the aim of establishing foreign venues for the sport of the British establishment. Their progeny have all but disappeared from the rivers at lower elevations, where the local people tend to fish for food rather than for sport, but they survive in the Nithi. Small, but plentiful, they still attract men with rod and fly.

We made a leisurely and rather late start from Urumandi, and Lloyfor surprised me by heading directly north, to the left of Mugi Hill, whereas both the map and my informant in Nairobi had indicated that the most direct route to Lake Alice was north-east, to the right of the hill. There could be no doubt about the hill itself. Mugi Hill is a steep-sided volcanic cone rising about 100m above the surrounding moorland; it is a prominent, indeed unmistakeable feature of the local landscape. But Lloyfor was the guide. I concluded he must know a better route and said nothing of my surprise. He set a cracking pace, and as our heading showed no sign of veering eastward, even when we were north of Mugi, I began to suspect some misunderstanding.

'This is the way to Lake Alice, is it?' I asked.

'Yes,' he replied, with sharp brevity suggesting that my question was impertinent, if not inane.

Forty minutes later we breasted a small ridge and looked down upon a lake. Lloyfor stopped. 'Lake Ayliss,' he said, with a sweeping indicative gesture of the right arm.

'Yes, Lake Ellis,' I replied, my suspicions confirmed. 'Where does the route for Lake Alice lead off from here?'

'This is Lake Ayliss.'

'No, this is Lake E-liss. I want to go to Lake A-liss. You said you know it.'

'I know Lake Ayliss. This is Lake Ayliss.'

I took the map from my pack and spread it before us. 'Lake E-liss,' I said, pointing to a blob north of Urumandi. I moved my finger north-eastward across a maze of grid squares and contour lines and pointed to another blob, 'Lake Alice, Lake A – liss,' I said. Lloyfor was perplexed.

'We are at Lake Ay-liss now. This is Lake Ay-liss, I do not know another Lake Ay-liss,' he said.

I realised, with a twinge of guilt, that he probably did not know much about map-reading either. 'Lake Alice is over there, under Ithanguni,' I said, pointing across the moorland to a distant peak.

The time was approaching noon; the map indicated that about 12km of rough terrain lay between us and Lake Alice. The question now was whether or not we could reach the lake in time for Lloyfor to return to Urumandi that evening, as we had planned. I was to stay at the lake for three nights and Lloyfor would return to help me carry out the gear on the fourth day.

Lloyfor dismissed the problem. 'We can make it,' he said, with a conviction that seemed to reflect determination rather than an assessment of what was involved.

We stopped to eat an orange on the high ground north of Mugi Hill, then plunged down through tussock grass into the Mutonga valley below. Then up through thickets of sugar-bush (protea) on the opposite side. The climb was steep. Once on the ridge, Lloyfor kept to the northern slope, which seemed a sensible strategy, for it promised to lead us directly to the high ground immediately above Lake Alice. But several watercourses intervened; and although only a couple of metres across, they were three or four deep and impossible to cross where we met them. Accordingly, we were forced to scramble up the steep shale slopes to the top of the ridge where, inevitably it seemed, we were confronted by more ridges, with more deep watercourses.

It was a demanding journey. I hardly need belabour the point. Pausing only for water and a puff or two at an amazingly durable cigarette he kept in his shirt pocket, Lloyfor maintained a stiff pace and brought us to the top of the last steep ridge close on five hours after leaving the roadhead. Lake Alice lay nestled in the depression below. 'It's completely hidden!' he shouted with spontaneous surprise.

From the rosewoods of Urumandi, the route to the summit (in cloud, top left) climbs
2000m through valleys, over rising moorland and steep mountain ridges.

Late afternoon at Lake Alice, and a rain squall sweeps in from the east.

We had covered at least 20km on our roundabout route to Lake Alice. Lloyfor ate another orange, accepted a hunk of bread, then set off on the shorter, but still not undemanding return journey while I carried my gear down to the lake shore. He was back at Urumandi by six o'clock, he told me later. 'Tired?' 'Not much,' he insisted.

As Lloyfor remarked, Lake Alice is completely hidden from view by the ridges surrounding it; in fact, the lake cannot be seen from any other point on the mountain. It lies in the eroded crater of Ithanguni, one of the larger subsidiary cones that erupted from the flanks of the Mount Kenya volcano during its 500,000 years of active life, 3.1 to 2.6 million years ago. The southern rim of the crater is a precipitous cliff rising nearly 300m above the lake to form the Ithanguni peak (3894m), but the remainder of the rim has been eroded down to a ridge barely 50m high on average.

The concealed location of the lake left it officially unknown until 1935, when its discovery was claimed by Mr K.C. Gandar Dower in the journal of the Royal Geographic Society.

Apparently Mr Gandar Dower had been in Kenya attempting to confirm the existence of a sub-species of lion, hitherto unknown to science, which was said to live like a leopard in the higher elevations of the Mount Kenya forest. He did not manage to find one, due to 'the difficult nature of the country and the rarity of the beast' but six months of searching and 'the inspection of two most enigmatic skins' convinced him that 'native rumours [and] the strange experiences of one or two white men' must be correct. The forest mountain lions retained their cub markings into maturity, and possibly were dwarf – with unusually shaped feet – Gandar Dower told readers of the RGS journal. Whether they were 'the last survivors of the original race, which was spotted, [or were] a throwback to the ancestral form,' he could not say. But he had discovered a lake.

It happened thus: in the course of searching for the mountain forest lion, some of Gandar Dower's scouts had seen a 'bean-shaped and very beautiful' lake on the high slopes of Mount Kenya above Meru, where none had been recorded hitherto. Doubtless spurred on by the prospect of failing in his initial objective, Gandar Dower decided to investigate. With donkeys, porters, and a Dutch companion, he set off from a camp at the forest edge north of Meru on February 26, 1935. The party traversed bogs and narrow gorges and saw some unfamiliar birds which the Dutchman identified as 'dugs'. Some days later, Gandar Dower realized 'that this identification was less a triumph of ornithological skill than a mispronunciation.'

When Gandar Dower and his party finally reached the lake under Ithanguni on February 27, 'the scene was a striking one,' he reports. 'The lip of the volcano curled around [the lake] in the shape of an amphitheatre ... clouds piled up from the south cutting out the sunlight. Dim streamers of mist floated between us and the summit of the cliffs. The sense of lifelessness became acute. The thin burnt scrub – forest fires too often sweep the mountain – the slabs of rock, the bleak colourless tussocks, an occasional giant lobelia or giant groundsel, made a chalice fit to hold these cold grey waters. There were no footprints by the margin, and no birds swam on the water.'

Gandar Dower refers to the lake as simply 'the lake' in his report and on an accompanying map, but it was subsequently referred to as Gandar Dower's lake, and ultimately, Lake Gandar. This was all well and good until Clarence Buxton, District Commissioner of Engare Narok in Masailand, came to hear of it early in 1937.

'I wish to protest against Mr Gandar Dower's claim to have discovered the lake to which he has given his name,' Buxton wrote to the secretary of the Mountain Club of East Africa. 'From the account I have read of Mr Gandar Dower's discovery it must be the same lake which I saw in January or February 1927 while climbing Ithanguni from Meru. I noted that the lake was not marked on the map and reported this fact to the Provincial Commissioner, Nyeri.'

Buxton concluded his letter with some information on the elusive mountain forest lion: 'While collecting heather for a bonfire on the top of Ithanguni an animal was seen which I described as being like a large snow leopard. It was about twice the size of an ordinary leopard and of a very light colour. Presumably it is the same animal as the one which Mr Gandar Dower calls a spotted lion ... '

But events had already overtaken Buxton's complaint. In 1936 the Mountain Club of Kenya had proposed that 'a lake newly discovered' should be named Lake Alice, after the Duchess of Gloucester, who had recently visited Kenya. The proposal was sent off to Buckingham Palace by airmail, and the secretary very soon received a reply from the Duchess's Equerry:

'I am directed by the Duchess of Gloucester to ask you to thank the President, the Committee and the Members of your Club for their kind suggestion to name one of the recently discovered lakes on the Northern side of Mount Kenya "Lake Alice".

'Her Royal Highness is greatly touched by their kind thought and has much pleasure in giving her approval.'

Unhappily, however, there was some confusion over the location of the lake in question. When proposing that the newly discovered lake should be named after the Duchess of Gloucester, the Mountain Club had, for some reason, recorded that it was situated in the Hausberg Valley on the eastern side of the mountain. The error was noted in 1938 and the secretary called a committee meeting: 'I gather Lake Alice is being identified in quite another quarter, somewhere near Ithanguni. One good reason being that there is in fact no permanent tarn in the Hausberg Valley.

'What I am afraid of is that the lake [now identified] as Lake Alice is the one already named as Lake Gandar! ... the one about which Clarence Buxton has already made a protest. The location of these lakes should have been confirmed ... It would not matter if the Duchess of Gloucester was not involved. We must identify a Lake Alice!'

A sub-committee on names for mountain features was formed and at its first meeting resolved that previous recommendations concerning Lake Alice should be rescinded forthwith, 'and that the large lake to the north of and immediately under Ithanguni be named LAKE ALICE, after HRH the Duchess of Gloucester; and that any other unnamed tarns shall remain nameless until such time as it is discovered whether there are any appropriate native names for them, or impersonal descriptive names are found for them.'

Subsequent surveys have confirmed that, yes, Lake Alice is the bean-shaped body of water lying immediately to the north of Ithanguni. Its precise position is 37 degrees 27 minutes east, and zero degrees 4 minutes south (just 8km south of the equator). The lake lies at an elevation of 3500m above sea level; it is 800m long, 350m wide and is oriented south-west to north-east along its length. A watercourse draining the face of Ithanguni enters the lake at the centre of the south-eastern shore, and the resulting accumulation of silt has narrowed the width of the lake at that point to give it a bean-shaped configuration. Eland frequent the lake, their hoofs leave deep holes in the marshy ground immediately above the highwater line.

Lake Alice fills the Ithanguni crater on the eastern shoulder of the massif.

Afro-alpine vegetation, including giant heather, everlastings and the occasional scarlet Mackinder's gladiolus, flourishes on the crater walls above Lake Alice.

The photographs of Lake Alice which accompany Gandar Dower's report of his discovery in the RGS journal show that its water-level was appreciably higher in 1935 than it is today. Perhaps by as much as a metre. Boulders which were partially submerged in his day, now stand high and dry. The shore is dry and sandy, with a rim of pebbles marking the highest reach of waves whipped up by the wind. The pebbles are generally no larger than a hen's egg, and the sight of them on a beach at that altitude can evoke memories of beaches elsewhere, but these are very different pebbles. They are composed of pumice, light as polystyrene. A handful thrown on to the water, floats, and drifts with the wind.

The pumice pebbles were a curiously disconcerting phenomenon. As indeed was the sound of swans flying by that I heard while walking around the lake on my first evening there. At least, I thought I heard swans flying by. The two-beat sound, best likened to the noise of someone breathing in and out heavily through half-closed lips, was exactly right; but by the time I had turned to look for the birds I remembered that the place was entirely wrong. I had been misled by memories of hearing and seeing swans fly over stretches of water in Europe, but this lake was much too high for them. Instructive, I thought, to note how the mind will so readily slot novel experiences among those already well-understood. But what was the noise? I heard it again that evening, coming from the direction of the Ithanguni cliff, but only when I was awakened in the night by the shriek of a hyrax did I realize that I had been listening to the call of a leopard. The animal was silent while it hunted, but I heard it each evening and found leopard droppings on a track under the cliff.

Lake Alice is an exquisite place. The lake is a light turquoise-blue colour in the shallows, gradually deepening to dark emerald-green. The water is soft and sweet and warm enough (by contrast with the frozen shore) for a morning dip, once the sun appears over the crater rim. Above the southern shore, where the beach is widest and whitest, a veritable meadow of tussock grass slopes gently up towards the crater rim. Dotted about the meadow, like parasols thoughtfully disposed about a lawn, are a number of elderly tree groundsels, strange relatives of the garden weed, found only on the high mountains of East Africa. The groundsels grow in candelabra form, up to four or five metres high, and each of their several branches is crowned with a cabbage-like cluster of leaves. The trees were in flower when I was there. A large stalk of vivid yellow flowers extended from the leaves at the end of each branch, attracting numerous sunbirds.

On my first full day at Lake Alice, I scrambled around the rim of the crater to the summit of Ithanguni (a slight rocky cone), and gazed happily at the pristine beauty of the lake and moorland spread out below. The distant peaks were clear, and seen from the top of Ithanguni, their prominence seemed diminished. On the second day, I fought my way through a tangle of shoulder-high heather, and over a rockfall to the foot of the sheer cliff beneath the peak, where I disturbed hyraxes and found evidence of the leopard I heard calling each evening. These bursts of exercise notwithstanding, however, I must confess that I found immobility the most satisfying form of activity encouraged by the warm sunshine and solitude at Lake Alice.

Given a pleasant location and enough to eat, indolence soon begins to seem a virtue at high altitude; one is inclined to let the mind wander – rather than the body. I was camped on the shore beneath the meadow and enjoying my visit enormously. In that happy state, laid back against the trunk of a tree groundsel with biscuits and beverage to hand, it was amusing to think about how the place might be adapted to provide for the enjoyment of larger groups. A lodge, tastefully designed, could be set on the slope above the meadow. Guests would arrive by helicopter; on nice days, they would be seated at tables arranged in the shade of the groundsels, and boardwalks laid over the tussocks would ease the difficulties of waiters serving breakfast. There would be a raft moored in the lake for the adventurous to swim out to, and trips to the top of Ithanguni for a picnic lunch. Lake Alice would become the most fantastic and most exclusive venue in Kenya. I could see it all, in the mind's eye … and I sincerely hope the vision never becomes more substantial than that.

Lloyfor arrived at my shoulder at about 10.30 on the morning of the fourth day, expected but unheralded, and offered me a hard-boiled egg. He had taken a more direct route than we had followed, but had been walking for more than four hours none the less. He drank some water, re-filled the bottle at the lake, took the pack, then led the way to the rim of the crater. Lake Alice dropped out of sight behind us, completely hidden again.

Following animal trails through the expanse of tussock grass to the west of Ithanguni, and into thickets of sugar bush lining the valley of the Kaziti stream, we came across a beehive set at chest-level on a tripod of branches. The hive had been made from a hollow tree-trunk, like those we had seen in the forest; the sugar bush was in flower and the bees very active. Lloyfor found three empty combs lying discarded a short distance from the hive. 'The owner was here yesterday,' he said.

Gathering honey in a national park is prohibited, but the attractions make it worth the risk. In the course of a year, a man can expect to take about 20kg of honey from every hive he sets up, Lloyfor told me, and the demand is such that a man with five hives can earn as much from the sale of his honey as does a petrol pump attendant working fulltime in Nairobi – and I know which job I would prefer.

We saw twelve eland on a ridge above the Kaziti, and a thirteenth, recently dead, lying where the trail led down to the stream crossing. Lloyfor tapped the head of the beast with his toe, and gestured to the rest of its remains scattered widely in the trampled grass. 'Lion,' he said. It must have been quite a tussle, but the ambush was well chosen. Thick scrub lined the approach to the crossing on both sides of the stream; steep banks led down to the crossing itself, so that animals entering and leaving it were disadvantaged by the physical exertion involved, as well as by the danger of predators lurking in the bush, waiting.

'But no lion now,' said Lloyfor, as though reading my thoughts. He clapped his hands as he led the way down to the crossing. 'Now they *must* go away,' I thought.

Lake Alice from the summit of Ithanguni, with Rutundu, another eroded subsidiary
volcanic cone, in the cloud shadow beyond.

The tussock meadow
and flowering tree
groundsels (*Senecio
battiscombei*)
above the southern
shore of Lake Alice.

A species of the common water plant *Potamageton* grows in the shallows of Lake Alice.
Fine glacial silts give the water its turquoise-blue tint.

Algae colour the water of a small unnamed tarn on a shoulder of the
Ithanguni crater, above Lake Alice.

Fire occasionally ravages the giant heathers (*Erica* and *Philippia sp.*) which grow at 3000m to 3700m on the massif, but regeneration is rapid and profuse.

The scarlet flowers of Mackinder's gladiolus (*Gladiolus watsonoides*) are frequently encountered among the tussocks and damp stony soils of the alpine zone.

Helichrysum brownei, one of the several species of everlasting flowers
which flourish throughout the alpine zone.

Tussocks in the shallows of Hall Tarns.

The alpine buttercup, *Ranunculus oreophytus*, grows on flat wet ground
in the alpine zone, between 3700m and 4300m.

The succulent *Sedum ruwenzoriense* is commonly found in the crevices
of raised rocky outcrops, from 3660m up to 4575m.

A blustery wind reveals the silvery velvet-like undersides of tree groundsel
leaves (*Senecio battiscombei*) in the Gorges Valley.

Tussock grasses, tree groundsels (*Senecio keniodendron*) and the ostrich-plume lobelia
(*Lobelia telekii*), on a high slope of the Gorges Valley at about 4200m.

Hall Tarns occupy depressions on a bluff high above the Gorges Valley, at 4297m.

CHAPTER EIGHT

Hall Tarns

Approaching Hall Tarns, still on the Chogoria route and east of the peaks, I saw three figures wandering back and forth across a meadow-like expanse of grassland in the valley below. They moved about independently, heads down, for all the world like golfers looking for a ball lost in the rough. I was travelling alone now, carrying an extremely heavy pack. These were the first people I had seen for several hours and their odd behaviour seemed a good reason to stop for a rest. I propped my pack against a convenient boulder and sat down for a drink of water and a bite or two of Kendal Mintcake, that essential ingredient of many mountaineering expeditions which is said to inject energy directly into the bloodstream – a dubious claim.

The figures in the valley were at least 500m away, but while I puzzled over the object of their search – rock specimens? rare plants? mushrooms? – a male voice of unmistakably American origin drifted up to me, clear as a bell. 'Hey, did you see that hyrax?' it drawled. The question appeared to elicit no response from the others, nor did the searching behaviour of the party change in any way. A lost golfball still seemed the most fitting, if least probable, explanation of what they were up to. We were all more than 4000m above sea level, and altitude does strange things to the mental processes, I mused. Since they were neither carrying packs, nor dressed for travelling, I concluded that they must be camped in the vicinity; probably at Hall Tarns, where I was heading. Fine. We would meet there, and I looked forward to the prospect of company that evening, and the explanation of their mysterious behaviour.

Meanwhile, cloud had enveloped the mountain, and sleet began to fall. Actually, 'fall' is the wrong word. The sleet blew horizontally across the landscape from the south, obliterating all sight of the valley below, and obscuring the trail ahead. I followed the cairns marking the route with particular care, never leaving one before the next was clearly identified; I was thankful they had been placed so close together, and could understand why: with distant views obscured, one could easily lose the trail across that flat, featureless plateau. The journey to Hall Tarns took longer than I had expected, and as I trudged through the sleet storm, well-protected against it, I began to think that the golfball-hunting party had been ill-advised to wander so far from their camp without adequate clothing. But when I finally reached the tarns I found no sign of them – only piles of rubbish marking the sites of many uninhabited camps.

Hall Tarns is a beautiful location – a group of five small mountain lakes poised high above the Gorges Valley – but its condition is a disgrace. The hut erected for the convenience of climbers intending to stay overnight is surrounded by a mess of tin cans, plastic bags and other, even less savoury items. Why is it that people who are prepared to carry provisions up the mountain, are unwilling to take the empty containers with them on the much easier return journey? And why don't they bury their excrement?

The only good thing I can say about the visitors who left so much evidence of their stay at Hall Tarns, is that they were content to eat and sleep among the rubbish. It was a relief to find that they had not sought alternative camping sites. Indeed, they appeared to have been decidedly unadventurous. While heaps of rubbish surrounded the tarn beside which the hut is situated, only a convenient pile of firewood testified to the previous occupation of an ideal spot I found next to the smallest of the tarns, just a short distance away. Hidden in a rocky depression, edged with bright green moss, and with tree groundsels positioned like stage props around a patch of dry level ground just right for a tent, the undefiled beauty of the place was particularly striking.

The sleet had stopped and the cloud had lifted soon after I reached Hall Tarns, but by the time I had found my campsite I was very weary indeed, and little able to appreciate the golden glow of sunset on the peaks, and the silver shimmer of ice beginning to form on the tarn. Once the tent was up, nausea suddenly forced me to my knees. My stomach heaved and ejected undigested lumps of Kendal mintcake. 'Altitude sickness,' I thought, but I believe exhaustion was the more likely cause, and have since been inclined to discount the energizing properties of mintcake. Not least because its sudden ejection left me very hungry indeed. As darkness fell (and the temperature with it), I ate a lot of cheese and salami, and drank several cups of rich, sweet chocolate before retiring to my tent. In cocooned comfort, I read a page or two by the light of a candle, then slept like a baby, as they say, for close on twelve hours. My capacity for sleep on the mountain never ceased to amaze me.

The Gorges Valley, on the high northern rim of which the Hall Tarns are perched, might seem to have been named for its topographical features, but in fact it was named by Halford Mackinder, the first man to reach the summit of Mount Kenya (in 1899), after Captain (later Brigadier-General) E.H. Gorges, who was District Commissioner at Naivasha at the time, and had helped Mackinder's expedition when they ran into some trouble with the local people.

The Gorges Valley is indeed a spectacular sequence of gorges, lined with massive cliffs and pitted with caves. The headwaters of the Nithi River flow through it, cascading over a series of splendid waterfalls which mark the step-like geological structure of the valley itself. From a rocky prominence known as The Temple, just south-east of the despicable Hall Tarns hut, the tail of the valley can be seen merging into the forest at Urumandi; in the other direction, westward, its head is seen to lie under the main peaks – Lenana, Nelion and Batian – a formidable array of rock and ice dominating the western horizon from that viewpoint.

The Temple is a sheer cliff, 300m high. At its base lies Lake Michaelson (also named by Mackinder, after a good friend who had aided his expedition). The lake is almost circular, about 400m across at its widest point, and enclosed by the steep cliffs of the valley walls. The stream draining the head of the Gorges Valley flows into the lake via a waterfall at the upper end, and out of it via another waterfall at the lower end. As with Lake Alice and the other high altitude lakes and tarns on Mount Kenya, the water of Lake Michaelson is emerald green – light at the edges, darkening almost to black as the water deepens.

From the vantage point of The Temple, the sight of Lake Michaelson lying below will encourage any visitor with a flexible schedule to consider making a detour to visit the lake – and perhaps even explore the valley and waterfalls beyond. Pristine is the word which describes its appearance from that distance most aptly. Glittering in the sunshine, surrounded to the water's edge by a dense green sward, the lake evokes images of Shangri La: a hidden place of comfort, magically encountered. It looks very welcoming – but there is an undeniable element of enticement in its welcome. Unlike the increasingly harsh landscape of shales and rocky ground which characterizes the route ahead, offering only the prospect of physical exertion and discomfort, the lake and the green valley seem to promise the certainty of a little more oxygen and an interlude of leisure. One might even consider the possibility of a swim.

Of course, the 'indolence factor' of high altitude environments is a major component of the attraction Lake Michaelson exerts. If time allows, the prospect of a sunny morning spent

Mist and rain or sleet frequently descend on Hall Tarns during the late afternoon.

clambering down to the lake and exploring its surroundings seems like an easy option. But beware. The jaunt is likely to involve rather more time and considerably more effort than was anticipated.

The scramble down to the lake begins immediately to the west of The Temple, where the sheer rock face merges into clays and shales which slope quite steeply, but negotiably, down to the valley floor. Ledges of short heather and grass have made a passable staircase of the slope, down which I leapt exuberantly. The sheer joy of going downhill swamped all sense of prudent concern about the difficulties of climbing up again, later in the day. As the sun rose above the peaks crowning the ridges to the east, the shadows they cast in the valley drew back like black velvet, unveiling expanses of tussock grass sparkling with frost; the stream meandering down the floor of the valley was lined with ice. Backlit by the rising sun, giant groundsels and lobelia (another giant high altitude plant with a common garden relative) stood prominently at declining heights on the slope, their positions marking changes in environmental conditions, just as does the succession of dominant tree species in the forest.

The river passes through a narrow gorge at the foot of The Temple, then tumbles down waterfalls to the lake. There is a route down on the north side of the falls, over a rockfall and through thickets of vegetation most memorable for the number of huge thistles encountered in their midst.

It took me about an hour to reach the lake shore from Hall Tarns, and then another 20 minutes or so to walk around the northern shore of the lake to the waterfall at its outflow. I did not hurry. At the outflow I sat on the bank and paddled my feet in the lake (the water was much too cold even to think of swimming). The view from that point was spectacular. The peaks, Nelion and Batian, were exactly framed in the narrow gorge created by The Temple on the north side, and the equally sheer cliffs of Macmillan Peak to the south. One side was in sunlight, the other in shadow, and the dazzling waterfall fell from the gap between them; the sky was deep blue and absolutely clear, but wisps of cloud were beginning to condense around the peaks. A light breeze riffling the surface of the lake died away momentarily, and the whole magnificent scene – waterfall and gorge, sky, cloud and peaks – was reflected on the lake. Then I noticed two figures approaching the lake shore from the direction of The Temple. I was immediately reminded of the people I had seen the previous afternoon, and, indeed, these were moving about in exactly the same manner: separate from one another, with heads down as though searching for something. They looked like the same people, no doubt about that, but now they were two, and yesterday they had been three. I had hardly thought of the group at all since noting that they were not camped at Hall Tarns; now I wondered where they had spent the night, and why had I not seen them earlier this morning in the upper valley, or near the waterfall, or at the head of the lake? They could not have been far away as I climbed down.

I pondered the mystery while putting my socks and boots on again and, on looking up, was very surprised to find it compounded by the fact that the two figures had vanished. They must have sat down for a moment, I decided; or were cooling their feet in the lake perhaps, as I had done. But no, I could not see them when I stood up. Then they must have gone behind a ridge, and would soon reappear. Wrong again. They did not reappear during the time that I stood looking. And then, as I scanned the landscape for a sight of the two figures, I realized that I was quite willing to believe that they were phantoms. This was an eerie thought, but appropriate to the mood induced by solitude at that altitude, in that environment – and thoroughly entertain-

The cabbage groundsel, *Senecio brassica*, is a low rosette plant which produces
a single flower-stem (top) before it dies.

Lake Michaelson, the Temple, and cloud obscuring the summit peaks beyond.

ing. I turned away and began scrambling down beside the outflow waterfall, determined – I now believe – that the reality of actually seeing the figures again should not be allowed to intrude upon the fantasy they had already conjured up.

Immediately below Lake Michaelson, the valley opened into a wide flat basin, which might itself have contained a lake at one time, since filled with silt and dried out. The vegetation included new species, and was noticeably denser than above. Scarlet gladioli grew among the heather stems on rocky ground; patches of cabbage groundsel, laid out as though by hand, exactly like cabbages in a kitchen garden, were disposed around the southeast-facing slope of the basin. And the basin itself was covered throughout with a thick growth of tussock grass. The mid-level of the Gorges Valley seems ideally suited to the needs of tussock grass – it grows prodigiously, which makes the place less than ideal for the easy passage of bipedal visitors.

Mice and eland can have no difficulty crossing a field of tussock grass, but for people it is an extremely wearisome undertaking. The solid portion of a well-developed tussock stands about half a metre high, and is surmounted by another half-metre of waving grass. Packed tightly together, like up-ended shaving brushes, an expanse of tussock grass confronts people wishing to reach the other side with a choice: either they can attempt to step from one tussock to another, or they can try to follow the narrow spaces that run like tortuous paths between them. Neither option is wholly satisfactory, and crossing an expanse of dense tussock grass inevitably becomes a mixture of the two. Exasperated by slow progress made by walking between the tussocks, you take to the tussock-tops, and after slipping off a few times, you follow the spaces between them again. In some instances, eland or other visitors may have made a good clear path through the tussocks, but there was nothing of this kind in the valley below Lake Michaelson. The tussock grassland was traversed only by the meandering river and its tributaries, and these, flowing fast and deep, were more of a hindrance than a help to progress.

I intended to climb out of the valley two or three kilometres further down, and return to my camp at Hall Tarns via the Chogoria trail on the northern rim. No tussocks up there, and as I stumbled on down the valley, I drew such comfort from the knowledge that the return journey would not be similarly impeded that I ignored completely the no less serious impediments of distance, elevation and rigour it would present.

I particularly wanted to see the Vivienne Falls, named after Vivienne de Watteville, the lady who had written about her stay at Urumandi, and surely worth the effort of struggling through the tussock grass on the valley floor above. But the falls, though about 100m high, are meagre in volume and the impression they make on a visitor approaching from the top is further diminished by the considerable difficulty of reaching a lower viewpoint. I had been told that a route down could be found to the south of the falls, but this seemed highly improbable as I began to seek a way through the rockfall and its covering of dense shoulder-high heather. Only when I had returned to the lip of the falls, and seen that none but rock-climbing (or hang-gliding) enthusiasts could find a way down the cliff to the north, did I accept the proposition that the south afforded a passable route. It was not so much the steepness of the descent that put me off, as the very obvious danger of slipping between the rocks. Over much of the descent, the rocks were covered with grass, shrubs and thick heather. A bushfire had run through the vegetation some time before, leaving charred dead stems and provoking a dense flush of new growth. The bush was now so thick that it was not always possible to see the rocky slope from which it grew,

Hill chat and groundsel at Hall Tarns.

and yet there were many crevasses to avoid – even the smallest of which might twist an ankle.

I carried an emergency pack – food, water, bivvy bag, extra clothing, matches and a whistle – but this was no place to be stranded alone. They say that so-called adventures only happen to those who are not prepared for every contingency, and descending the slope beside the Vivienne Falls I seriously feared that I might be in for an adventure. I was relieved, therefore, when I safely reached clear level ground some distance from the foot of the falls. It was after one o'clock, so I sat down on a rock in the shade of a tree groundsel and had some lunch. The wind was rising, I noted, blowing down the valley from the peaks. A cold wind, turning the leaves of the groundsels to show their silvery undersides, and sending waves of movement through the tussocks. Cloud was gathering over the valley to the west.

By this time, I had descended about 750m below the elevation of Hall Tarns, and would have to climb that much in the course of an 8km trek back to camp. It does not sound an excessive undertaking, but when the climb begins at over 3500m, altitude adds a debilitating dimension.

I left the valley nearly 2km downstream from Vivienne Falls, where the northern wall of the valley begins to lie back a little, and offers a less precipitous – but still steep – route to the rim. From valley floor to rim at that point is a climb of 300m; I tackled it in a series of shallow zig-zags – nothing too strenuous – and on reaching the top was amazed to note that the exercise had taken the best part of two hours. But I was not alarmed. I found the track from Chogoria almost immediately and, turning to head west on that familiar ground, felt that the rest of the trip would be an easy stroll back to camp – which indeed it might have been, had the wind been warmer, less strong, and blowing from behind rather than into my face. A greater reserve of energy would have helped too; my pack seemed extraordinarily heavy.

I have a theory concerning walking speeds on high mountains: if the pace makes you breathless or causes muscles to ache, slow down; you are going too fast. Accordingly, my progress along the track to Hall Tarns was slow, and I took frequent rests out of the wind. But the theory is founded on the assumption that there is plenty of time available, and that congenial walking conditions will persist. Before very long I could see that neither of these assumptions applied to the present journey. The hands of my watch were moving much faster than the ground was moving beneath my feet. A single short pace for every panting inhalation and exhalation simply was not enough. Furthermore, the clouds were thickening ahead, and the wind striking my face brought flurries of sleet with it.

By five o'clock both the weather and my physical condition had worsened. I began calling on relatives and friends to send some energy – telepathically. None recalls having received the message. Cloud and sleet had reduced visibility drastically and made even the well-trodden trail difficult to follow; I lost it finally in a broad marshy depression where I could see no cairns. The trail had seemed to leave the depression by way of a short steep rocky slope, but at the top I found clear untrodden gravel – and no sign of a trail. The map indicated that the tarns were little more than 1km away to the west, but following the compass in that direction led me straight to the edge of a steep ravine. I cut back north for what I judged to be a similar distance, then turned west again. This time I soon fetched up against a steep ridge, which I had neither the inclination nor the energy to surmount. North again, and before long I was looking into another ravine. This made no sense at all – ravines to north and west, and a high ridge in between – none of them indicated on my small-scale map. I thought of returning to the depression and searching for the trail again, but I was not at all sure that I would find either, nor did I have much energy for the search.

Casting about my small circle of visibility, in a landscape with no recognizable features, where even my own footprints were difficult to retrace, I eventually had to admit that I was lost. What is more, the light was rapidly fading and I must find some shelter for the night. I was cold, dismayed and exhausted. Then the cloud lifted. Just like that. One moment I was completely enclosed, the next I could see the peaks and knew exactly where the tarns lay. And although a night in the open would have been an appropriate culmination to the day's 'adventure', the sudden realization that I would be able to spend it in my tent and sleeping bag after all was no anti-climax. The sense of relief and joy I felt is inexpressible. Within minutes I found the trail again, and half-an-hour later I was at the tent. It was completely dark by then, and ice already coated the flysheet.

The landscape above Hall Tarns, with cloud clearing from the peaks.

The summit peaks, Nelion (left) and Batian, seen from the trail above Hall Tarns.

CHAPTER NINE

Kami Hut

I was drinking tea before the sun rose on the morning I left the tarns, and shook ice from the flysheet before packing the tent. It was a glorious morning – clear and perfectly still. From Hall Tarns, the route to the peaks crossed a broad plateau of rocky ground. Giant groundsels lined the route; small ridges were minor challenges which I surmounted with ease, gratefully reassured of the ability to move about and carry a load. The peaks lay dead ahead. Nelion and Batian, flanked to the south by Lenana.

In contrast to the predominantly grey and dusty green shades of the surrounding land-scape, the peaks are a light chocolate-brown colour. A tracery of deep shadows and startling white patches of ice and snow defines their massive, fractured structure. Sheer cliffs, huge slabs, tall columns, vast crevasses – the visual impact of the peaks seen by a climber approaching from Hall Tarns is sobering. Hitherto, it was possible to think of the peaks as simply a part of the whole mountain. But no longer. Now they dominate landscape, time, and all ambition. They rise so steeply from the ridge ahead – and so far above it. The rock looks so precariously balanced, one huge block upon another; the snow and ice looks so ephemeral, and the summit looks simply improbable – a cluster of boulders at an elevation usually reserved for clouds and aeroplanes. And gazing wonderingly at the summit, the ambition to stand on those boulders suddenly seems more improbable still. The ultimate aim of the expedition, cosily unheeded in the green depths of the forest and in the folds of the moorland, is now starkly revealed. Climb that! What a conceit!

More than a twinge of self-doubt intruded upon the pleasure of the morning as I trudged across the plateau from Hall Tarns, looking up to the peaks; and I found my pace falling readily into the rhythm of the words running through my head: improbable, impossible, improbable, impossible ...

The incline is gradual for the first part of the journey, gaining little more than 100m over a distance of about 2km, which allows the muscles time to warm up and gives the eye and the mind plenty of time to contemplate the reality of the peaks and the climb that lies ahead. At an elevation of 4400m the trail steepens dramatically, the last vestiges of plant life are left behind and the surface underfoot changes from hard-packed gravel and rock to loose scree. Walking is no longer so easy. The feet tend to slide away beneath you, and each step requires not only the effort of raising the weight of the body that little way up the mountain, but also the effort of kicking the boot into the scree to give it some purchase. A line of cairns marks the route leading directly to the top of the slope, but upward progress between them is best achieved by a series of wide zig-zags – which of course multiplies the total distance covered several times over.

The arduous monotony of the ascent is broken by a succession of rocky prominences which provide something stable to sit upon, the excuse to rest and perhaps even to admire the splendid view of the tarns and the Gorges Valley broadening out beneath. Looking upward, some of these prominences are large enough to fill the skyline and can thus inspire a hope that the top of the slope is nigh. But it is a false hope. When you reach one, there is always another beyond – until you reach the last one, though by then the lesson of previous disappointments is likely to have induced a despondent resignation to the unremitting effort of the ascent. Striving upward, panting, one step after another – there is never enough oxygen, never quite enough energy, and precious little fun. And this is how it will be from now on, I thought.

I arrived at Simba Tarn in just such a mood: any pride in the achievement of what had gone before significantly reduced by the prospect of what lay ahead. Resting against a boulder on the slope above the tarn, I looked down at the Gorges Valley, the moorland and the forest far beyond. Ithanguni (with Lake Alice hidden in its crater), Urumandi and Chogoria lay down there, days away. This distant view evoked some pleasing memories of the recent past, but they belonged to another world and hardly impinged upon my contemplation of the immediate future.

Simba Tarn is a small oval-shaped body of water, surrounded by black sand, shattered rock and boulders. It lies on a shoulder of Lenana's northern flank at an elevation of just under 4600m. Simba is the Kiswahili word for lion, and the tarn acquired this improbable appellation in 1924 when porters accompanying two climbers, Dutton and Melhuish, on their route via the tarn insisted that a lion also had passed that way. Dutton and Melhuish denied the possibility. A lion could not have reached that elevation, they said. A leopard perhaps, but not a lion. The porters remained adamant, however, and eventually the climbers conceded the point (though not without a touch of exasperation), and the tarn became known as Simba Tarn.

Subsequently, this questionable report of a lion high on Mount Kenya doubtless became one of the tenuous pieces of information which inspired Gandar Dower's search for the spotted mountain lion, as recounted in chapter seven.

From Simba Tarn I had planned to cross over the col (named Simba Col, after the same enigmatic lion) into Mackinder Valley, where I would spend a night camped at Shipton's Cave (Shipton made the second successful ascent of Mount Kenya, in 1929, thirty years after the first), before climbing out of the valley again on the south side and walking around the peaks to the head of the Teleki Valley, where my ascent of the peaks proper would begin. While dreaming up these plans I had imagined that I would reach the cave with time and energy to spare for exploring that area on the same afternoon. I thought I might look for the skeleton of an elephant, known as Icy Mike, which lies over the northern rim of the valley at about 4400m, and even considered the possibility of climbing Terere or Sendeyo, two outlying peaks directly to the north of Shipton's Cave, while I was in the vicinity.

These plans had seemed perfectly reasonable from the comfort of an armchair in Nairobi. Seated on a rock above Simba Tarn, however, they seemed outrageous. The rigour of the climb that morning, combined with the memory of my experiences down the Gorges Valley and on the journey back to Hall Tarns, two days before, convinced me that serious reconsideration was called for. I crossed over Simba Col and down to an outcrop overlooking the valley for an assessment of what was involved. The view was spectacular, and the undertaking I had planned formidable indeed – not only in what I had intended to do after reaching Shipton's Cave that afternoon, but also in the plan to climb out of Mackinder's Valley next morning. The prospect was all too reminiscent of the return from the Gorges Valley, with the added concern that the intended journey was longer, steeper, and would begin at a higher elevation than the one already undertaken.

Meanwhile, across the head of the valley to my left, little more than 1km away as the crow flies (though only eagles and ravens fly at that altitude) and just 200m below my present elevation, I could see the aluminium walls of Kami Hut glinting in the sun. Kami Hut was no

Simba Tarn.

particular attraction in itself, given the very real probability of it being as badly neglected as the hut at Hall Tarns, but the Mountain Club of Kenya had erected another hut nearby, primarily to serve as a base for mountain rescue operations, but also for the use of mountain club members. I knew that the MCK hut was equipped with a table, a bench, bunks and foam mattresses; it offered a warm, comfortable night, and I had the key in my pocket. Furthermore, a popular route around the peaks led from Simba Tarn, over the northern ridge of Lenana and across the lateral moraine of the Gregory Glacier to the Kami Hut.

Cloud was beginning to gather around the peaks and swirl about the head of the valley, promising a damp afternoon in any event. With little reluctance, I decided to abandon my original plans and take the direct route to the MCK's Kami hut instead. I turned to recross Simba Col and join the track from there, and was startled to see a solitary figure with a pack on his back and a ski-stick in each hand striding purposefully to the top of the col. We were about 100m apart, but he was ahead of me, and disappeared over the col before I reached the top. I expected to find him resting beside the tarn as I had done, and even looked forward to a word or two of conversation. But when I came in view of the tarn there was no sign of him, neither resting beside it nor crossing the landscape beyond.

I found the figure's sudden disappearance distinctly unnerving. The rational explanation must be that he had taken the track down towards Hall Tarns, or had joined the trail around the peaks, heading either south or west, but there was no sign of him in any direction, and I was unwilling to believe that he had been moving fast enough to cover the distance which would have taken him out of sight in the time available. Of course, I now realize that I was estimating his progress according to my own meagre pace, but this did not occur to me at the time. Eventually I had to acknowledge that some rational explanation must apply, but I remained puzzled by the man's sudden disappearance, none the less. Not least because it reminded me of the three figures I had seen near Hall Tarns, and the two at Lake Michaelson. Now I had seen a solitary figure at Simba Col.

This sequence of mysterious encounters has the makings of a good and scary gothic tale — one in which the narrator ultimately is engulfed by the events of the story he relates. Back here at sea level, the idea certainly has some appeal, but up there on the mountain, in chilling solitude and already over-awed by my circumstances and enfeeblement, such an idea seemed nothing short of appalling. But it came to mind very readily indeed, closely followed by the fear that dwelling on it might tempt fate to turn fantasy into reality: three, two, one, zero — and then I would disappear too.

After a scramble up the slope to the west of Simba Tarn, the route to Kami Hut is all downhill, and occasionally of a gradient that made me very glad I was not going the other way. The lateral moraine of the Gregory Glacier, for instance, is very steep indeed. The moraine is an irregular pile of silt and rock debris squeezed out from beneath the glacier as it advanced down the mountain, grinding out the concave face that now comprises the head of the Mackinder Valley. The glacier itself has since retreated, leaving its moraines clear of ice and standing as prominent evidence of its previous extent.

The glaciers on Mount Kenya have advanced and retreated with the changing pattern of world climate over the millennia. Glaciologists estimate that during the ice ages, the glaciers on Mount Kenya may have extended down to about 3000m, which is the present upper limit of the forest. In modern times they have been retreating steadily. The Lewis Glacier, the largest body of ice on Mount Kenya, which lies on the south side of the ridge between Point Lenana and the main peaks, is now less than half the size it was in 1893 when it was measured (and indeed, named after an American geologist) by J.W. Gregory, a British geographer and the first man to reach the glaciers. The snout of the Lewis Glacier extended down to an elevation of 4465m in Gregory's day; now it is above 4600m. The snout of the Gregory Glacier has retreated even higher than that of the Lewis, and presently lies at about 4700m. The Gregory was, of course, named after the geographer, but not by him. Gregory, in fact, never saw the glacier which bears his name though it lies on the north side of the same ridge from which the Lewis Glacier falls to the south.

The glacier was shrouded in cloud as I followed the trail to Kami Hut, but its proximity was very evident. The air was damp and bitterly cold; pockets of ice and snow lay along the trail down the moraine, and among the jumble of rocks which marks the former course of the glacier. Where the trail leaves the valley, vegetation is suddenly evident again — indicating not only more congenial climatic conditions, but also an environment less susceptible to the landslides and rockfalls which frequently scour pioneering plants from the head of the glaciated valley. The ubiquitous tree groundsel, wiry grasses, low scrub bushes and the occasional everlasting flower were a welcome sight. Over a last heap of boulders I saw the aluminium Kami Hut, and a short distance from it, the MCK hut – also a metal rondavel construction, but clad with a layer of black creosoted boards for added insulation and protection. I was cold and very tired by then and not at all keen on further activity that day — no matter what contingency arose. It was with some foreboding, therefore, that on approaching the hut I noticed not one, but two very stout cylinder locks securing the door, while I had only one key in my pocket. For a moment I feared the worst — and could hardly think of anything worse than being locked out of the MCK hut. But the fear, though intense, was short-lived. My key opened both locks and very soon thereafter water was heating on the stove and I was stretched out on a five-inch-thick foam mattress — bliss, sheer bliss.

The MCK hut at Kami Tarn stands at 4439m on a high northern shoulder of the mountain, with Nelion, Batian and a string of subsidiary peaks ranged close behind, and the Mackinder Valley stretched out below. It is a magnificent site. The hut is primarily intended to provide a dry, windproof and properly-maintained base for rescue operations on the northern side of the mountain. Happily, such emergencies occur infrequently and the hut is more often used by MCK members as a base for recreational climbing. The comfort it offers is little short of luxurious — and promises to become more so. There is even a large kitchen sink stowed under the bunks, apparently awaiting connection to a pipe from the tarn above the hut. One suspects that final installation of sink and water supply is delayed only by the problem of the water freezing in the pipe each night; but this difficulty will be overcome in due course, I have no doubt. Meanwhile, hats off to the band of club members who erected the hut. They all deserve a medal.

Surveying the large prefabricated panels of the hut and the thick exterior timber-cladding; the smooth cement floor, the stout timber bunks, the shelving units (not to mention the kitchen sink), one does wonder how the materials were transported to the site. The component parts of the aluminium hut at Kami were dropped from an aircraft, and badly bent in the process, which is one reason why the hut sections do not fit together properly, and why the interior is more thoroughly ventilated than is necessary at that altitude. But the components of the MCK hut

Kami Hut, with cloud swirling around the summit, 750m above.

were brought in by mules, via the Mackinder Valley, and the hut was erected by club members on weekends and holidays.

I was refreshed, body and soul, and gazing in awe at the peaks glimpsed through breaking cloud at a distinctly unrealistic elevation above the hut when two heavily laden climbers arrived. Introductions identified them as Max and Minoru, German and Japanese respectively, but both based in Germany and serious climbers with considerable experience of alpine peaks. The Eiger, Weisshorn, Mont Blanc – that sort of thing. None the less, they looked dreadful at the Kami hut, and readily admitted that they felt dreadful too.

'The altitude,' Minoru explained apologetically, though his outline of their efforts over the past few days left me feeling that they had very little to apologize for.

They were planning ten days or possibly even two weeks of climbing on the mountain, during which they intended to reach the summit by a variety of routes – each more difficult than the last. They had ascended via the Naro Moru route and the quantities of equipment and provisions required for ten days or two weeks of serious climbing had obliged them to make the journey from the roadhead to Mackinder's Camp at the head of the Teleki Valley not once, but twice. They had established a reserve store at Mackinder's Camp and brought only essential equipment for this first assault on the peaks. Even so, they had taken seven hours to reach Kami from Two Tarn, a trip generally reckoned to take less than three.

Minoru complained of a splitting headache and aching limbs; Max was more stoic and said nothing about his condition, though his gaunt face and sunken eyes suggested that he felt no better than his companion. They both appeared to be at risk of imminent collapse, I thought, and definitely in need of good food and plenty of rest. I was impressed, therefore, when they began discussing their plans for the next day. A climb up the western edge of the Gregory Glacier and across the ice to scale Lenana from the north side would take care of the morning, they concluded, and perhaps leave time for an assault on one of the minor peaks in the afternoon. On the day after they would tackle the north face of Batian, and following that they intended to move to the southern base of the peaks for an attempt to scale the Diamond Couloir – one of the most demanding routes on the mountain.

Clearly, these were men whose scale of accomplishment I could hardly credit, let alone hope to emulate – or match. I was reluctant to say much of my modest plans, but when I answered their polite enquiry with the information that I would be climbing Nelion and possibly Batian from Austrian Hut in the company of Iain Allan, they misinterpreted my modesty and seemed to assume that Iain and I would be tackling one or more of the severely difficult routes to the summit. Iain Allan is one of three men set to become a legend of climbing on Mount Kenya in modern times (the others are Ian Howell and Phil Snyder). Collectively, and occasionally in the company of others, these three men have pioneered more new routes on Mount Kenya than any other climbers – some of frightening severity. The ascent of the South-West Face, for instance, first climbed by Iain Allan and Ian Howell in 1977, takes three days but offers no ledge wide enough to sleep upon; hammocks strung from pitons hammered into the face must be used instead.

'What will you be doing with Iain Allan?' Max asked.

'I'm not entirely sure,' I replied, and this was perfectly true. I was far from sure what I would be doing with Iain Allan; or even if it was a good idea to think of doing anything at all with him.

I believe Max then understood that my mountain-climbing experience was limited. He was kind enough not to make a point of it, but did leave me feeling that he would have made fuller use than I of the opportunity to climb with Iain Allan.

'We wrote to the Mountain Club from Germany, and tried to contact Iain Allan in Nairobi,' he said wistfully, 'but had no luck. So we will climb alone.'

Minoru rested most of the afternoon and evening, but Max spent much of the time seated on a rock, studying a map of the peaks and peering up into the shifting clouds above. Towards sunset, the cloud cleared, exposing the peaks as cruel-dark pinnacles of rock silhouetted against the western sky. And as the cloud drifted from the peaks above, the Mackinder Valley below filled with its soft vaporous billows. Veils of cloud, lightly orange-tinted by the setting sun, drifted across Terere and Sendeyo and up to the head of the valley – it made a splendid sight.

'It reminds me of the Dolomites,' Max murmured as we gazed down the valley. 'When the sun is setting they turn red and look just like that. It is very beautiful. I like the mountains very much. I like to climb them.'

I left Kami Hut at seven the next morning, and by ten was slouched against a boulder 100m or so from Two Tarn Hut, enjoying a rest and some sunshine. The trail had taken me over two cols of around 4600m at the head of the Hausberg Valley, and was almost entirely in the shadow of the peaks at that time of day. It had been a chilling journey, both in terms of temperature and the icily unforgiving quality of the environment. Now I was sitting in the sun less than an hour from the luxurious appointments of another MCK hut at Mackinder's Camp. The hard part of the day was over, the rest of it was all downhill, so to speak, and I was particularly looking forward to devouring a can of tuna fish and several slices of fresh bread, thickly buttered, these being the most immediately appealing options among the provisions awaiting me at the hut. Then two figures appeared from over the ridge behind Two Tarn Hut. They entered the hut and emerged some minutes later bearing what appeared to be bags of rubbish – though this seemed unlikely. As they turned in my direction I waved. They strolled across to me and we exchanged greetings. They were national park rangers, based at Mackinder's Camp, and they were indeed collecting the rubbish which visitors always leave behind. Rangers from the Mackinder's Camp station regularly clear rubbish from the huts around the peaks, but not from Hall Tarns, they explained when I remarked upon the deplorable state of that place. Yes, it was very dirty, they agreed, but it should be cleaned by rangers from Urumandi.

'Have you come from Chogoria?' they asked me.

'And you are going to Mackinder's Camp?'

'Yes.'

'Then I will help you,' one of them said as I stood up.

'But this pack is very heavy,' he muttered as he attempted to swing it on to his shoulders with the ease that his nonchalant manner seemed to require.

Twenty minutes later, with the Mountain Club Hut now visible at the base of the ridge, no more than half-an-hour away, I suggested that perhaps he had had enough and would like me to carry the pack for the rest of the journey. He agreed.

'It is very heavy,' he said again as I took the pack. It was indeed heavy, and his acknowledgement of the fact boosted my morale considerably. After all, I thought, he should be more able to carry a heavy pack at that altitude than I. My acclimatization programme had produced

Two Tarn Hut with the summit beyond.

some effect, it seemed. Perhaps reaching the summit of Mount Kenya was not such an improbable ambition – perhaps it was even possible.

I did not weigh my pack while I was on the mountain or preparing for the trip. This was not an oversight, but it was not exactly a conscious decision either. It might have stemmed from some superstitious fear that actually knowing the weight of the load would have a detrimental effect on my ability to carry it, but I think it most likely that I did not weigh the pack simply because there was little point in doing so. It contained only essential items; I would have to carry everything, however much the pack weighed. Since returning home, however, I have re-assembled and weighed the load – just to put some measure on what I remember as a rather strenuous bout of exercise. The full pack – with tent, sleeping bag, stove, photographic equipment, clothes and food for eight days – weighed 28kg. The pack I carried on days out of camp – with emergency gear and clothing, cameras, water and a little food – weighed 12kg.

Climbers on the trail above Mackinder's Camp.

The Diamond Couloir route leads directly to the summit via the notch between Batian and Nelion.

CHAPTER TEN

Top Hut

When I left Max and Minoru gazing up at the peaks from Kami Hut I had not expected to see either of them again, least of all on a stretcher. Four days later, however, at the Naro Moru roadhead where I was assembling supplies and equipment for the climb with Iain Allan, a group of porters arrived carrying a stretcher – in rather jaunty fashion, I thought – and the occupant was Minoru.

He was in considerable pain; a falling boulder had struck his knee with great force the previous afternoon; the joint was grossly swollen and he feared that the bones had been broken. Their climbing programme had been going well until then, he said. After successful forays from Kami Hut they had moved round to tackle the Diamond Couloir and had established a bivouac at the base of the climb. They had planned to begin their ascent early next morning, and decided to spend the rest of the day on the lower part of the route, testing the ice and their technique – though without ropes. But the afternoon is a very dangerous time to be climbing on the lower part of Mount Kenya's steep glaciers, for by then the sun has had time to melt exposed parts of the upper reaches and so precipitate ice- and rockfalls. Minoru was caught in one such fall. He was lucky that it was a relatively minor one, and that the boulder had struck his knee, leaving him able to hang on, rather than his head or chest, where it might have killed him and certainly would have knocked him off the glacier.

With Max's help he had slid on his backside off the ice and hopped down to the Mackinder's Camp ranger station. Now, after 24 hours of continuous pain and physical stress, he was worried about the availability of adequate medical care, and was also distressed by the demands of the porters who had carried him down the mountain. There were 16 of them, and each was expecting to be paid a sum equal to a week's wages for the day's work. This amounted to $320, not a lot, perhaps, when measured against the value of saving a knee, but more than Minoru had with him in ready cash. He would have to get the money, he said. Where was the nearest bank? When would it be open? And he would need proper receipts from the men, witnessed by some recognized authority, in order to claim against his travel insurance. Could they do that at the Naro Moru police station?

But the men did not want to call at the police station, nor did they want to wait for their money until Minoru had been to a bank. The scene was like a black farce – the men shouting and gesticulating, Minoru lying in the stretcher at their feet, hurt and exhausted. Apparently, however, his plight was little different from that of many climbers who have been injured but not rendered totally immobile on Mount Kenya. A team of expert climbers from the Mountain Club is always on call for rescue operations that involve dangerous rock climbing or the use of ropes, but all others are handled by national park rangers and transportation from the peaks is left to the mercy of the porters.

This is not to suggest that the porters are anything but merciful. Their concern for injured climbers such as Minoru is fully evident, but they are freelance operators, not employed by the national park or any other authority from which they can claim payment. Not unnaturally, therefore, their concern for the injured party is matched by an insistence that someone must pay for their humanitarian services. The rescue may be a matter of life or death to those being

119

rescued, but for the rescuers it is just a job. And over the years, the job has encouraged them to adopt a rather critical view of the people they help. Firstly, they have seen that by far the greater number of accidents on the mountain are the result of inexperience or inadequate preparation. Most accidents should not have happened. Secondly, they have found that although all injured climbers welcome the service of being carried off the mountain, not all are so willing to pay for it when they reach safety. Many protest that rescue is the bounden duty of the national parks authority, if not even a contractual obligation of charging climbers an entrance fee.

When I tried to explain Minoru's point of view to the porters, insisting that he was an honest man, they immediately suggested that I should pay them on his behalf, and collect the money from Minoru at a later date. My first response was to protest that I did not have that much money to hand either, and then I remembered Max. Why had not he escorted his injured companion off the mountain, and thus been there to deal with the porters and ensure that Minoru received adequate medical attention with a minimum of delay?

Max had not wanted to abandon the climb, Minoru explained, and besides, there was equipment to be retrieved from the bivouac they had established at the base of the glacier. So Max planned to climb the peaks alone, collect the gear on his descent, and meet up with Minoru again at their hotel in Nairobi. This all seemed a trifle selfish and lacking in proper concern, but Minoru insisted it was quite in order. He would have done the same, he said.

I last saw Minoru as the porters bundled him into the lorry that would take him down the 26km of rough forest road to the police station at Naro Moru, and then another 40km to the hospital in Nyeri, but I have since learned that his injury was not as severe as he had feared, and the porters were paid.

The route from the Naro Moru roadhead to Mackinder's Camp ascends 1200m in a distance of roughly 10km. It begins at an altitude of about 3000m, ends at 4200 m., and the guide book suggests that the average person, carrying an average-sized pack, should allow between five and six hours for the journey. I carried my light pack (of average weight) while a porter, Steve Menja, carried the bulk of the gear, and we reached the Mountain Club hut at Mackinder's Camp four hours and ten minutes after leaving the roadhead. I was immensely pleased with myself, and if that sounds immodest I can only plead that the memory of Minoru's fate on the peaks, combined with the prospect of attempting to scale them myself had left me in dire need of something to boost my morale.

The route climbs firstly through a narrow belt of forest (a pale shadow of the forest on the Chogoria route), then scales a broad ridge of marshy tussock-grass moorland known as the 'vertical bog'. The name is apt, for the terrain is steep (though far from vertical) and very often sodden, so that visitors are obliged to wade through mud and scale a series of miniature waterfalls as they ascend, but this day it hardly seemed steep at all and was completely dry. Dust rose underfoot. At about 4000m there is a convenient resting-place on the crest of the ridge above the Teleki Valley which affords a wonderful view of the peaks. This is the first sighting of the peaks at close quarters for many climbers, as testified by the number of discarded film cartons among the sundry picnic rubbish scattered about the place.

From the ridge, the path descends gently along the southern wall of the valley, through thickets of giant groundsel and lobelia (definitive specimens of the curious plants have been neatly labelled), and ultimately down to the Naro Moru River, which it follows to Mackinder's

Batian and Nelion (centre), Lewis Glacier and Point Lenana (right), Mackinder's Camp (lower left).

The numerous hyrax which live among the boulders around Mackinder's Camp subsist on natural
vegetation and titbits provided by visitors.

Camp at the head of the valley.

A number of buildings have been erected at Mackinder's Camp for the benefit of climbers. A crude stone bunkhouse accommodates package safari customers, and a nearby rondavel is used by their porters. The national park ranger station is less obtrusively set among the rocks, almost out of sight, some distance from the bunkhouse, and the Mountain Club hut is situated amid a tumble of boulders at the edge of the valley floor. The peaks and the southern glaciers rise sharply above Mackinder's Camp, and although the clutter of buildings and human activity is often regarded as a deplorable intrusion upon the pristine beauty of the mountain, there is also a case for claiming that the grandeur of the peaks is actually enhanced by the incongruity of the puny structures that have been erected for the benefit of people wishing to climb them. For one thing, the buildings give a sense of dimension and scale that is otherwise missing. Size and distance are notoriously difficult to judge in a pristine mountain landscape. Without some recognizable object against which to assess the size and proximity of a peak, a weary climber might be inclined to assume that the peak appears to be so large only because it is close by. Such assumptions can be comforting, but they also can be cruelly misleading. Mountains are usually even larger than they first appear to be and much, much further away.

The lessons of hard experience will very soon correct any tendency to misinterpret size and proximity, but there is no chance of it arising on the approach to the peaks via the Teleki Valley. The buildings at their base look like boulders or minor rock piles, and could be mistaken as such from a distance, were it not for their square edges and regular appearance. The scale is awesome. The peaks are so huge and rise so high while the buildings – the conceits of human endeavour and ambition – are such insignificant dots on the landscape below. If those tiny buildings are, say, three metres high, then how much higher must a person climb to reach the summit of the mountain that soars above them? The answer is over 1000m, and many hours of very arduous and occasionally very dangerous climbing.

I read, drank many cups of tea and ate half a cold roast chicken on the day I spent at the Mountain Club hut. I also watched the many hyraxes which inhabit the immediate vicinity of the hut, and saw a trail of leopard footprints on the path to the river. I wondered if it was the same leopard which had recently attempted to remove a sheet of corrugated iron from the roof of the ranger station, presumably in search of something to eat. Rangers were sleeping in the station at the time, and the leopard was only briefly deterred by the noises they made when they woke up. It returned to the roof and its effort to get in, time and again, but succeeded only in giving the rangers a very restless night.

In the evening, a short rotund figure arrived at the door and introduced himself as Thumbi Mathenge – the very man I had been wanting to meet, as they say. Thumbi is one of a small and elite band of rangers with experience of technical rock-climbing on Mount Kenya; he had accompanied Phil Snyder on the first ascent of the Diamond Couloir in October 1973 and had been a member of the mountain rescue team Snyder had formed and trained during the 1970s. Thumbi was wearing his orange mountain rescue team anorak – much faded and not a little frayed, as the team itself became after Snyder left in the late 1970s. Its members were transferred to other national parks; Thumbi went to the Aberdares National Park; John Omira found himself obliged to work as a ranger in the Marine National Park at Watamu, on the coast. The break-up of the rescue team was part of what was termed the re-organization of Kenya National Parks, though disorganization is a more accurate description of what ensued on Mount Kenya and in other parks – neglect, poaching and corruption became rife.

In 1987, Perez Olindo, a former Director of National Parks, and another casualty of the re-organization, was re-instated with a brief to get the parks back on the rails. By 1988 there were signs of progress. Thumbi and Omira had returned to Mount Kenya, but the Park's mountain rescue facilities were still some way down the list of priorities.

Thumbi laughed when I said that I had heard a great deal about him, and had been hoping we would meet, but he did not take the remarks as a invitation to conversation, as I had intended. He refused my offer of tea and asked of my plans. I told him I would be meeting Iain Allan at Austrian Hut, on the edge of the Lewis Glacier, the next afternoon, and climbing Nelion and possibly on to Batian as well, with him the following day.

'That's good. Then I think we will meet on the mountain,' he said.

'You will be climbing too?'

'Yes, I will be climbing,' he replied. 'Early tomorrow morning. A man died on Nelion yesterday and we must bring the body down.'

This was shocking news.

'He fell?'

'No, he had a heart attack at the top of De Graaf's Variation on the Normal Route. Then he died.'

The man had been an American visitor, Thumbi went on. After he had died, the man climbing with him had descended immediately and gone to inform the next-of-kin from Nairobi, leaving the park authorities to arrange for the body to be retrieved. Of necessity, the man would have been lying on the ledge above De Graaf's Variation for two days and nights before he was brought down. Somehow, the thought of the man having been left up there, dead, was very disturbing indeed – not frightening, or ominous, or even discouraging to my own forthcoming climb, but simply not right.

There was little more to say. Thumbi maintained a jocular camaraderie as we parted, but our mutual good wishes and expressions of looking forward to seeing each other again 'up there' were rather forced, and probably entirely inappropriate.

I thought of the task he faced – fetching a dead man from halfway up a climb that is rated difficult to severe in the technical scale of these things. I thought of the poor fellow himself – dead, and frozen by now, in such a cruel and lonely place. And I thought of my own intention to climb the peak – in the company of a highly experienced climber, admittedly, but with no personal experience of rope-work and the technical rock-climbing that was involved. We would be climbing the Normal Route (via De Graaf's Variation, for all I knew), which offers the most straightforward and 'easiest' ascent.

But 'there is no easy route to the summit of Mount Kenya,' Iain had said. 'The Normal Route is just the least difficult, that's all.'

Steve and I made a leisurely start from Mackinder's Camp next morning, and by the time we reached Austrian Hut at 10.15, Thumbi and his companions had already begun lowering the body from the ledge above De Graaf's Variation to the base of a prominent rock spire known as Mackinder's Gendarme. Against the face of the mountain, the figures looked no bigger than ants on a kitchen door. Even with the aid of binoculars they were difficult to see and, at that distance, the foreshortened perspective eliminated all indication of there being ledges for them to stand on, and left the impression that they were crawling across the face of the rock, rather

The giant cabbage groundsel, *Senecio brassica*, thrives at over 4500m in sheltered aspects. Algae and suspended glacial silts colour the water of Teleki Tarn (left).

Emergency. A man has died on Nelion. The minute figures of the party retrieving
his body can be seen just below centre-left.

than clambering about on it. Their progress seemed pitifully slow, but this too was partly a distortion that distance brought to the scene: whatever their speed, the scale of the distance they covered was greatly diminished by the vast areas of rock-face surrounding them.

Incongruously, the bright orange rope on which they lowered the body was often more plainly visible than the men or the body itself. Its movement – a swinging, short straight orange line – caught the eye more readily against the background of fractured rock than did the amorphous figures at either end of it.

By three in the afternoon, Thumbi and his companions had completed about half the descent and their dangerous task had assumed the character of a macabre sideshow. As I watched from the comfort of a sheltered, sunny spot on the ridge above Austrian Hut, refreshed by snacks and an occasional hot drink, and joined from time to time by porters and groups of package-trip climbers on their way to or from Point Lenana, or going around the peaks, it was sometimes difficult to retain a proper sense of what was going on up there on the south-east face of Nelion: right before our eyes, Thumbi and two others were actually risking their lives to recover the body of a visitor who had died on the mountain. What obliged them to take the risk? The parks authorities provided virtually nothing in the way of essential equipment – just two ropes, already old and their remaining useful life indeterminate. Such slings, pitons, carabiners and harnesses as Thumbi and his companions were using, were their own personal property, given to them by visiting climbers who appreciated the necessities of the service they were endeavouring to provide on the mountain.

Around three o'clock, while the retrieval party were dealing with the difficulties of lowering the body over the snags and buttresses of a portion of the route known as One O'Clock Gully, a large group of porters arrived from Mackinder's Camp with a stretcher on which they were to carry the body down to the roadhead. They joined me on the ridge, and were amused to point out that the heap of rocks near which I had chosen to sit was actually the grave of a man who had fallen off the mountain and died a few years before. He and his companion had fallen when the rock to which their rope was attached had broken away, they explained. The other man was buried near the face from which they fell. Buried is not the right word. There is no ground at that altitude in which bodies can be interred. When next-of-kin advise that they do not want their dead relatives returned to their homelands, the bodies are simply laid out in shallow depressions and covered with rocks – with as much attendant ceremony as can be mustered. The heap close to me on the ridge was little more than a metre high; the body could not have decayed much in that environment – in fact it was probably deep frozen. Thirty climbers have died on Mount Kenya in the past 50 years, of whom a dozen are buried on the mountain.

With these sombre thoughts in mind I retired to the hut for a cup of tea. Shortly thereafter, my reverie was disturbed by the entry of a couple who greeted me in strident English heavily overlaid with a Middle-European accent. I assumed they were a man and a woman, though in fact there was little about them which justified the distinction. Stature, voices and clothing were identical, only the softer facial skin of the one who did most of the talking suggested a female physical structure. Their manner was brusque and condescending. While gathering together the belongings they had left in the hut while climbing Nelion, they told me there had been an accident on the peak.

'The dead man?'

'No, not the dead man. We helped the rangers with him on our way up the peak this

127

morning,' they replied, somewhat dismissively. 'This is another man. He was climbing solo and fell on One O'Clock Gully; we helped him down to the top of the scree. He says his ankle is broken. This is his boot, he had to take it off.' And they placed a boot and some other items of the man's equipment on the hut shelf.

I immediately thought of Max. Was it him?

'No,' they replied, 'the German climbed yesterday, solo, then went round to fetch his equipment from beneath the Diamond Couloir. This man is American. He cannot get back on his own. You must go and help him cross the glacier. We must get down to Mackinder's before dark, and will send porters up for him – if there are any.' And with hardly a farewell, they departed.

I returned to the ridge, certain that I would be foolish to attempt to go to the American's aid, as the couple had instructed. Iain should be arriving soon and he would be far more capable than I – but then selfish considerations impinged (mixed with feelings of guilt in equal parts): what would happen to our plans for tomorrow, if Iain became involved with a rescue operation today?

From the ridge, I could just make out the figure of the American edging his way down the scree towards the glacier. His progress was slow and looked painful. The porters waiting to carry down the body were watching his progress, and that of the retrieval team above, with an astonishing lack of concern. I suggested that they should go and help the American cross the glacier, and then take him down to Mackinder's in the stretcher.

'No,' a spokesman replied adamantly, 'we have come for the body. The stretcher is for the body.'

'But the body is dead,' I insisted, 'the American is still alive, and he needs help.'

They talked among themselves for some minutes, in the vernacular, in a manner suggesting that the discussion of whether or not they should help the American was at a close. The body took precedence, it seemed, presumably because the fee for its recovery had already been negotiated. Then three of them stood up and announced that they would go and help the American. And money? they asked their colleagues. Plenty, one replied.

I do not know if the three negotiated the terms of the American's rescue before they began to help him down the rest of the scree and on to the glacier, but they spent 20 minutes with him before commencing the descent, and I could think of no other reason for the delay. It was past four o'clock by then, the scree was in shadow and the temperature dropping rapidly. The injured man surely was in no state to strike a bargain.

Intemperate thoughts concerning porters and the morality of rescue were at the forefront of my mind when Iain arrived, but his sympathies were entirely with the porters. He had very little time for the many inexperienced, inadequately equipped and over-ambitious climbers who come to Mount Kenya and then expect to be rescued when they get into difficulties, and no time at all for the inexperienced, inadequately equipped and over-ambitious climber who attempts to scale the peak on his own. As we watched the porters help the injured American to hobble across the glacier, Iain's attitude seemed a little hard on the man. After all, we did not yet know whether he was inexperienced, inadequately equipped and over-ambitious or not. I thought we should reserve judgement, and give him the benefit of the doubt in the meantime. But Iain was absolutely right.

When the American finally hobbled into the hut supported by two porters I could only

The lone American climber who fell and broke an ankle on One O'Clock Gully
is helped over the treacherous Lewis Glacier by porters.

The top huts, with the Lewis Glacier and Point Lenana beyond. The commodious Austrian Hut was a gift
from the Austrian mountaineering fraternity following a rescue of their colleagues
who fell while climbing the peak in 1972.

wonder at the conceit which had persuaded the man he was capable of climbing the peak, and well-enough equipped to do it alone. And what reserves of strength, courage or ambition had taken him up several long and dangerous pitches to One O'Clock Gully where he had fallen? If other climbers had not found him, and helped him down, he would have been stuck there for the night – and possibly much longer. He could have died there.

He was in his late thirties, a tall reasonably fit-looking man whose moustache and weather-ed face could have made him a good candidate for one of those cigarette advertisements which feature men of virile appearance in rugged environments. But he was woefully out-of-place on Mount Kenya. And very poorly equipped. Levis are fashionably tight and hard-wearing, but provide little warmth when the temperature drops. A broad-brim hat keeps the sun out of a man's eyes, but does not adequately keep his ears and his head warm. He wore a loose, waist-length zipped jacket, and a copy of the popular Mount Kenya guide book protruded from its pocket. He carried a camera, but no rope or climbing equipment was evident.

Despite the cold (it was now after five o'clock), the man's hair was wet and his forehead glistened with sweat. He drank gratefully from the water-bottle we offered, and transferred its remaining contents into his empty bottle, remarking that he had had nothing to drink for quite a while.

Outside, the porters were preparing the stretcher for the American's descent, apparently having decided to leave the body for collection another day. But they could not decide upon the best means of getting him down the 700m scree to Mackinder's Camp. Should he hobble down with the support of a porter under each arm, or should he be strapped into the stretcher and carried down?

When asked, the American chose to travel in the stretcher. But once the straps were the tightened he found the pressure on his unprotected ankle intolerable, and said he would prefer to hobble down. He leaned heavily on the shoulders of two porters, but then found that their shorter stature did not raise his injured ankle above ground level. To avoid knocking the dangling foot against the rocks, he had to hold it lifted behind him as he hobbled forward – an impossibly tiring endeavour. After covering no more than 10m the American gave up and took to the stretcher again, grimacing.

At last the journey of relief seemed about to begin – but not just yet. As the stretcher team reached the top of the ridge, some 30m from the hut, another group of porters arrived from below. They had brought a second stretcher with them, and apparently expected to carry down the live man while the first group should take the dead body. As the two groups met on the ridge, the injured man was lowered to the ground, and left there for more minutes than I care to recount while the two groups milled around him and haggled over which should carry him down. The hapless fellow lay at their feet, immobile, wide-eyed, looking up at the noisy rabble as they shouted at one another, argued, laughed loudly and finally agreed to exchange roles.

The stretcher and its bearers disappeared over the ridge in the last glimmer of daylight. Thumbi and his companions arrived at the hut minutes later. It had taken them eight hours to get the body down from De Graaf's Variation to the base of the climb, and they had left it lying at the top of the scree. Their manner was subdued – and not only by exhaustion. The task of manhandling more than 80kg of, quite literally, dead weight down the precipitous face of Mount Kenya, nearly 5000m above sea level, does not inspire lively conversation. They said little as they sat drinking tea in the hut.

Meanwhile, the porters outside had concluded that they could not cross the glacier to fetch the dead man that evening, but would go down to spend the night at Mackinder's Camp and return for the body next morning. Noisily, they disappeared over the ridge. Shortly thereafter, Thumbi slipped off to follow them. We had not noticed his departure until Iain suggested that we should ask Thumbi if he would climb with us the following day. This seemed a very good idea to me, but would it appeal to Thumbi, after the day he had just spent on the peak? Probably, Iain replied, if I would pay him well. I would, but where was Thumbi? Iain rushed from the hut and caught up with him on the ridge, where they agreed on a fee for the day equal to about half his monthly wage. We heated and shared out the chicken stew that Iain had brought with him, and drank mugs of hot chocolate. The sky was perfectly clear, the air was thin and the night was intensely cold – even within the hut, where the stove and our bodies must have raised the temperature a few degrees.

'We're now as high as the summit of Mont Blanc,' Iain remarked, 'but still a good way from the top of Mount Kenya.'

Iain had intended to give me a lesson in the rudiments of rock-climbing that afternoon, on the ridge above the glacier, but events had eliminated all opportunity of that.

'In fact, there isn't a lot I can teach you in advance,' he said when we spoke of the omission. 'There's only one rule in rock-climbing: you have four points of contact with the rock – two hands, two feet – and no more than one of them should ever be detached from the rock at any one time. That's the only rule – all the rest is experience.'

We retreated from the cold into our sleeping bags shortly after eight o'clock. With the candles out, the interior of the hut was brightly illuminated by moonlight streaming through the window. From where we lay on the upper sleeping platform, we looked directly on to a landscape which reminded me of the pictures sent back from Mars by the Voyager spacecraft. Black sky, sparkling bright stars, and a foreground of broken rock and inky shadows. Cold, lifeless and distinctly uninviting. And yet, perversely, that view gave me the first surge of excited anticipation that I had experienced on the mountain. Hitherto, I had taken my pleasures as they came, enjoying the moment and deliberately avoiding contemplation of what the next day might bring – largely because I could only be certain that it would bring more physical hardship. Now I felt differently. I suddenly realized that despite the warnings and the fears, despite the evidence I had seen of injury and death on the mountain, I was actually looking forward to climbing it next day.

Whatever might be the result of my attempt, I shall never be better prepared to climb Mount Kenya, I thought. Carrying a heavy pack for several days had made me reasonably fit, and I was very well acclimatized. I had no headache, and no nausea. I had been sleeping well and knew I would that night too. Furthermore, and probably the greatest advantage of all, I was going to climb with Iain Allan and Thumbi Mathenge. I remembered the words of another of the mountain's legendary figures – Phil Snyder.

'If you can't actually envisage yourself standing on the summit of a mountain, you won't ever get to the top. You have to be convinced you can do it.'

I was convinced. I could see myself standing on that cluster of boulders at an elevation usually reserved for clouds and the passage of aeroplanes.

The south ridge and summit of Nelion from Top Hut. A late evening view of the morrow's challenge.

Iain Allan has climbed on Mount Kenya more than 150 times, and has pioneered many outstanding routes.

CHAPTER ELEVEN

Nelion

Iain wanted to make an early start. He set his alarm to waken us at four o'clock, but it failed to operate and we slept very soundly until five, then lay awake for several minutes, awaiting our morning call, before we realized that the time had passed. The realization provoked no rush to recover lost time, however, and such a relaxed start surely augured well. It was a tranquil morning, and the calm silence of the mountain in the pre-dawn hour fostered an optimistic frame of mind.

We filled our water-bottles at the Curling Pond, a small frozen tarn lying a short distance from the hut, whose edges seem permanently thawed, clambered across the upper end of the ridge on which I had spent much of the previous afternoon, and slithered down to the edge of the Lewis Glacier. But this was not the solid river of ice that popular imagery encourages one to expect. It had none of the hard and permanent quality conveyed by the massive blue-green glistening icewalls of the Rhone Glacier, for instance. No, the edge of the Lewis Glacier we confronted that morning looked more like a heap of frozen snow cleared from an industrial site. The ice was dirty, and porous. The surface was pock-marked with stones and grit, the core held quantities of pulverized rock, and melt-water streamed from its fissures and crevices.

The total volume of Lewis Glacier is about 10 million cubic metres, and it covers about 300,000 square metres of the steep slope between Point Lenana and the main peaks. These dimensions are minuscule by global standards, but location alone makes the glacial zone of Mount Kenya unique. It lies just 17km south of the equator. The glaciers have formed where the fierce heat of the equatorial sun is countered by low ambient temperatures and enough precipitation to create ice – but their existence is a precarious affair. As summer and winter alternate between the hemispheres, the northern and southern glaciers on Mount Kenya are alternately struck by and shaded from the equatorial sun – and they grow or diminish accordingly. During northern summers, little or no snow accumulates on the northern glaciers, and a good deal of melting occurs, while the southern glaciers can become deeply covered in snow. The situation is reversed during the southern summer. In some years the snowfalls may consolidate and replace the ice that melted during the previous summer, but the trend this century shows an overall decline in the size and volume of the glaciers – winter snows do not match summer thaws.

We were climbing in late January, when the Lewis Glacier was exposed to the full effect of the southern sun and devoid of snow cover; the surface of the glacier thawed each day and froze overnight; the steep slopes were slippery as glass; puddles of water collected on the level terraces, awaiting the misplaced foot under a thin skin of ice. At close range, the tiny glacier's proportions seemed monumental and its condition treacherous – not at all the sort of terrain the uninitiated would venture on to with an easy mind – especially not in the half-light of dawn, when shapes are deceptive and distances difficult to judge.

Thumbi noted my hesitation. 'Take this,' he said, handing me the ice-axe he was carrying.

You must hold the axe by its operative end and stab the spiked handle into the ice on the upper side of you, I recalled as I cautiously followed Iain and Thumbi on to the glacier. If you slip, you must hang on to the handle with both hands, keep it upright and push the spike into the ice; thus it will act as a brake and halt your slide down even the steepest slope – so they say. The principle sounds simple enough, and any one of my first steps seemed likely to test its efficacy as I attempted to abide by the cardinal rule for crossing steep icy slopes: you must always lean away from the slope, never towards it. This, of course, contradicts the natural tendency to lean inwards and put out a hand for something to hold on to if you slip, and it requires a conscious effort to put so much faith in the soles of your boots – particularly on an icy surface which offers little grip. But then glaciers offer few if any handholds either. You must lean out, keeping the centre of gravity as high as possible. The logic is obvious – if you lean in towards the slope, your feet are likely to slip out from beneath you and you will be testing the braking efficiency of the ice-axe in no time – but surprisingly difficult to follow.

I relied on the soles of my boots whenever the rough frozen surface seemed to offer adequate grip, but cautiously stabbed the ice-axe spike into the slope on the upper side whenever it was close enough. My progress was slow and occasionally uncertain, but creditable enough, I thought. Iain, meanwhile, showed how experience makes light of difficulty. He skipped across the ice, balletically, his balance enhanced by speed and his progress hindered only when he stepped unwittingly into a knee-deep pool of melt-water. Thumbi proceeded in a more stately fashion, his steady progress and demeanour more indicative of a resolute determination to achieve the aims we had set ourselves, than of any pleasure he derived from the exercise.

It was daylight by the time we stepped off the glacier. Iain led the way up the scree and stood waiting for us at the rock face where the climb begins. As I approached, he called down: 'You can go round that way, if you want,' and indicated a route through the boulders to my left.

I looked ahead, and saw why he had suggested a deviation. The body lay a few metres further on, blocking the trail.

I saw no point in trying to avoid the body for the sake of my own sensitivities, but as I drew closer, a sense of impropriety developed and intensified in a manner that I can only liken to the increasing resistance that is felt as you attempt to bring the identical poles of two magnets together. It was not right that we should have met like that. He surely deserved more respect than his death and our arrival allowed.

The dead man had been wrapped in a dark grey blanket, and trussed with an orange rope for the recovery. During the descent, the blanket had slipped from his head, exposing bushy eyebrows, closed eyes and part of a deeply lined face. He lay on his right side, and might have been asleep, inadequately wrapped in a thin blanket, except that he was lying with his head down the slope. And that was especially disquieting. No one could sleep comfortably with their head so far below the level of their feet, and it seemed quite wrong for a dead man to have been left in that position. And the hands. Protruding from the blanket close to his head, they were rigid, contorted, the fingers stiffly bent as though still fastened to some crucial hold; and they were a deep grey-blue colour, almost black.

As we joined Iain at the rock-face, I asked Thumbi what I should do with the ice-axe, which would not be needed on the climb.

'Leave it down there,' he replied, pointing in the direction of the dead man, 'It belongs to him.'

But I did not feel inclined to approach the body again, so I stood the ice-axe against the rock face directly above it.

The climb begins above the scree on the far side of the Lewis Glacier.

We roped up. Two ropes, each about 50m long, both joined to Iain at one end and one to Thumbi and one to me at the other. They were attached to harnesses that fitted around the waist and between the legs, rather in the fashion of an infant's swing, so that we would be supported upright, rather than dangling, should we ever find ourselves suspended at the end of the rope. When we were ready, Iain gave me a quick run-though of customary climbing procedures.

'On belay!' the leader would call out when he had reached the top of a pitch and fastened himself and the rope to a piton hammered into the rockface, or to a sling fixed around a firm and reliable outcrop.

'Take in!' the second man would then shout, followed by 'that's me!' as the rope drew taut, and 'climbing!' when he began to ascend the pitch. As the second man climbed, the leader would take in the rope across his shoulders, and stand prepared to take the strain of a fall. It sounded straightforward enough.

Iain began climbing almost exactly from the spot where we had made our preparations, though it seemed to Thumbi – and certainly to me – that the rock a few metres to the right offered an easier first pitch: ledges like a staircase, rather than an almost vertical groove with an awkward-looking protrusion blocking the route two-thirds of the way up.

'I can get up here all right,' Iain replied when Thumbi invited him to consider the alternative. And indeed he could – like an overgrown spider monkey – his arms and legs moving up the rock in meticulous co-ordination, with hardly a pause. I recalled the rule about only one of the body's four points of attachment being detached from the rock at one time, and now I could see what Iain had meant when he said that everything else is experience. He never appeared either uncertain or insecure. He moved – no, flowed is the word – up the groove and over the obstacle like oil defying gravity; never once appearing to be anything less than totally attached to the rock, but always moving upward. 'You have to go for it,' he explained later. 'If you keep moving you'll most likely come through. Stop and you're stuck.'

He disappeared over the rim of the ledge above, and shortly thereafter the words 'on belay' rang out. Now it was my turn.

'Can't we go up there?' I asked Thumbi, indicating the easier route.

'We must follow the same route,' Thumbi replied, just as I had thought he would.

'Take in!' I shouted, and the rope snaking up the pitch drew taut to the clip on my harness. 'That's me!'

I reached up to grasp two obvious handholds, and raised my right foot to a small ledge at about thigh-height.

'Climbing!'

The first six or seven metres were no more difficult than scrambling up large boulders on a beach; both hand- and footholds were easy to find and progress was rapid and unimpeded. But then I found myself turned sideways in the narrowing groove and stuck below the outcrop. I had to get over it – but how? Both hands gripped firm holds on the rock to the right of the groove; my right foot was placed equally firmly on a convenient small ledge, and my left foot was nicely wedged in the groove itself. I could hardly have been more securely fastened to the rock, and could move any one of my four points of attachment with ease, but I could see no place for either hands or feet that would carry me up and over the obstacle above.

I remained in that position for some time, raising one foot, then another; leaning back, stretching up – trying to find a way out of my predicament, and becoming increasingly alarmed by my inability to do so. But Thumbi was keeping an eye on my progress and, like every good instructor, he waited until I had tried all the options I could see before telling me what to do next.

'Bridge!' he shouted from below.

Bridge?

'Get your left foot on to that step out on the rock there. Now get your right foot up on to the ledge that side.'

I did so, and miraculously found myself standing astride the groove, 'bridging' it with a foot on either side, rather than stuck within it. The position was precarious but felt surprisingly safe. Though standing on ledges only a couple of centimetres wide, with legs wide apart and a straight drop below, I could lean my elbows on the troublesome rock jutting from the groove, and reach for good handholds above it. With no difficulty at all, and a good deal of relief, I clambered on to the rock and followed a succession of small bumps and ledges – no more than finger- and toe-holds some of them, but all perfectly adequate – to the belay point. So that's what 'bridging' can achieve. My gratitude to Thumbi was boundless.

'That was pretty good,' said Iain, clearly not intending to devalue encouragement with any excessive use of superlatives at this early stage. But I thought it was bloody marvellous! I was a little out of breath, perhaps, but also elated and not at all scared or awed by the first taste of the enterprise we had embarked upon: 18m done, more than 300m to go. Or, to put it another way: we had just climbed the equivalent of a modern six-storey building, and now confronted the Eiffel Tower.

The terrace on which Thumbi soon joined us afforded a easy stroll to the left before delivering us at the foot of a gully known as the Donkey Walk. No one can suggest a reason for it being so named. Emphatically, it is not a gully you could persuade a donkey to ascend – walking, or by any other means. I clambered up the gully behind Iain – an easy 25m climb (the height of an eight-storey building) which bolstered the confidence I had gained on our first pitch. Thumbi followed, and we mounted a series of ledges leading up and across the face to the right.

Though there was usually plenty of room on each ledge, there was often a fair drop beneath. Thumbi stood on belay, paying out the rope as Iain advanced across the face. Iain used carabiners – D-shaped clips – to fix the ropes to slings hanging from pitons hammered into the rock-face, or to steel wire loops with a solid metal attachment which was wedged into small cracks. The rope was attached to the rock in this way every two or three metres, so that if any of us slipped on the rock, he would fall no further than the distance from the last fixed point. Iain secured the ropes as he advanced, we unclipped them as we followed, and Thumbi retrieved the slings and carabiners as he brought up the rear.

Iain was dressed in what I believe should be called his Patagonias – in the linguistic tradition which brought the Persian word for a pair of everyday trousers into the English language as the name for what the Oxford Dictionary describes as a sleeping suit – pyjamas. Patagonias, however, are a suit of thermal underwear, made of capilene polyester (an improved manmade fibre currently replacing polypropylene in the outdoor clothing industry, I am told) and marketed under the name Patagonia by an American company. They are comfortably loose-fitting, with natty elasticated cuffs at neck, wrist and calf, and come in three grades of insulation against the cold – light, medium, and heavy. Iain found the medium grade of this

On the south-east face of Nelion. An easy traverse before negotiating the Keyhole.

underwear perfectly adequate for climbing on Mount Kenya in fine weather, and donned the outer clothing he carried in his pack only if conditions deteriorated.

The Patagonias Iain wore on our climb were a bright, almost incandescent red, and his outfit was topped off, as it were, with a thermal ear-hugging cap of lapis blue. He cut a striking figure as he moved confidently and effortlessly across the face, and his absence was all the more noticeable when he abruptly disappeared behind a large block at the end of the traverse.

Iain's progress always engaged my rapt attention and admiration. He made everything look easy, but when he moved out of sight behind the block I was left contemplating exactly what my own progress entailed. By now, we were almost exactly above our starting point. The ropes snaked above the ledge and followed Iain around the block. The block itself jutted from the face and seemed to hang directly above our starting point; I deliberately avoided looking down, but have a distinct recollection that a climber falling from the block would very soon land beside the corpse awaiting collection at the foot of the cliff – and in even worse condition. A piton might come loose, a sling might break, a rope might snap – any technical failure could turn a slip into a deathfall. Such thoughts do arise, and then I heard Iain calling from the other side of the block:

'On belay! Now this is a really interesting bit,' he announced encouragingly.

Interesting? I could think of more appropriate adjectives.

'It's called the Keyhole,' Iain's disembodied voice went on, 'get out to the corner at the end of the ledge and you'll see why.'

I shuffled along the ledge towards the corner, unclipping my rope as I advanced, very grateful to note that Iain kept it taut all the while. At the corner, there was little but the rope to hold on to, and no more ledge to stand on. I could not see around the corner, nor could I see any way of moving forward. The smooth rock simply ended at the corner and, with a sheer drop below, the position was very similar to that which people threatening suicide confront when they take to a window ledge on a high building – nowhere to go but down. Iain was still out of sight.

'Are you at the corner?' he called out.

'Yes.'

'Look down to your right, and you'll see a small ledge jutting from the rock – it's about a metre from where you're standing now.'

I looked down to my right and sure enough, there was a small ledge – looking very small indeed against the precipitous cliff that fell away beneath it.

'I see it.'

'Right. Now this is the clever bit,' Iain called out, apparently having decided that progress was more likely to be encouraged by arousing enthusiasm than by attempting to diminish the difficulty of the next step. 'You must get your right foot out on to that ledge ...'

But I couldn't do that without moving my right hand as well – the ledge was too far out. What about the one-and-only rule of rock-climbing: only one hand or foot should be detached at any one time? Before I could ask, Iain went on:

.'.. and as you move your right foot, you must slide your right hand round the corner. You'll feel a handhold, a really good one that you can get your fingers into and pull yourself around the corner. That's the keyhole. It unlocks the climb.'

Lunging across empty space, from one relatively sound foothold to another offering rather less security, while simultaneously reaching around the corner of the rock for a handhold you

The top of One O'Clock Gully affords a splendid view over the Lewis Glacier to Point Lenana and beyond.

cannot see, is a movement that requires an act of faith. Quite apart from the danger of falling off, it is an all-or-nothing movement. Once begun, it has to be completed. The entire weight of the body shifts on to the right foot as you lunge, and I am not at all sure that I – for one – could have regained my former position once I had left it. But faith is easily summoned when you are following another climber, and are attached to him by a rope that he is holding taut. I lunged and reached and found the handhold. It was as firm and secure as a drawer-handle, and big enough to wrap your fingers around. With my weight on the hold, I brought my left foot down, changed footing, raised my right foot to a higher step and hauled myself on to the ledge above.

A deep sense of relief and achievement ensued, and with it an opportunity to contemplate the achievements of the men who had first climbed Mount Kenya. Negotiating the Keyhole brought us to a platform at the foot of Mackinder's Chimney, a narrow, steep, daunting cleft in the rock face, tall as an average ten-storey building, which Mackinder and his two Alpine guides had climbed in 1899 and which Shipton and Wyn Harris ascended in 1929. Mackinder makes no specific mention of the chimney in his account of the climb, but his rope still hung in it when Shipton and Wyn Harris made their ascent. The rope was too frail to use, but its presence indicated that ascent was at least possible, and this was a tremendous encouragement to the two men. Shipton led the pitch and, in a short paragraph describing that part of the climb, even he admits to 'struggling for some time below the overhang' in the chimney.

Looking up from the platform, Mackinder's Chimney appeared to consist of nothing but overhanging blocks of rock, streaked brown, black and grey. The end of a rope suspended from the top would hang two or three metres clear of the face at the bottom. The pitch is rated IV – very difficult or mild severe – on the scale by which mountaineers assess climbs, and it was evident that the ascent would require rather more skill, physical prowess and faith than I possessed. I was therefore relieved to learn that we would be taking an alternative route, and Thumbi was puzzled, not to say put out, when Iain announced that the alternative route was not via the Rabbit Hole, as Thumbi had expected, but via a rib immediately to the right of it.

After my experience on the Keyhole, the very name – Rabbit Hole – conjured up dire images of difficulty if not distress ahead. While Keyhole could only have metaphorical connotations, it seemed quite likely that Rabbit Hole might be a passably accurate description of what confronted climbers seeking some way of avoiding the rigours of Mackinder's Chimney. I remembered Ian Howell's story of the difficulties he encountered while attempting to pass through the Rabbit Hole with a stack of polystyrene tiles for the summit hut on his back. The tiles, being almost weightless, were strapped to Ian's back in a stack which extended some distance above his head, but man and tiles could not pass through the Rabbit Hole together, Ian discovered when he got there. Climbing alone, without a rope, the contortions required to remove the tiles from his back and manhandle them through the hole hardly bear thinking about, though Ian makes an amusing tale of it. But then, Ian Howell has climbed the peaks more than 150 times, often solo – including thirteen ascents carrying the prefabricated parts of the tiny summit hut that the tiles were to insulate. Thumbi had climbed via the Rabbit Hole many times too, and he insisted that there was no easier route. But Iain was adamant – and right, as it transpired, for when we reached the ledge at the top of Mackinder's Chimney Thumbi readily admitted that climbing via the Rabbit Hole was more difficult.

But difficulties on a mountain are always relative, I thought as we scrambled up One O'Clock Gully, where the American had fallen, and not a little related to the prevailing weather conditions I might have added, as I basked in warm sunshine for fifteen minutes or so while Iain laid out the ropes across the traverse leading to the base of Mackinder's Gendarme. I was actually enjoying the climb, and that realization came as something of a surprise.

Mackinder's Gendarme is a sharp pinnacle of rock which stands almost precisely where the southern ridge of the mountain joins the upper wall of Nelion. Mackinder and the Alpine guides, César Ollier and Joseph Brocherel, had pitched a tent at the foot of the Gendarme on 12 September 1899, and spent the night there, in preparation for their successful ascent of Batian next day; Shipton and Wyn Harris had rested there long enough to catch sight of Kilimanjaro, 320km to the south, when they made the first ascent of Nelion on 26 January 1929, and on 30 January 1988, Iain Allan, Thumbi Mathenge and I stopped there to rest and eat an orange. The time was nearly 10 o'clock.

'We're doing really well,' Iain announced, with only a faint tone of surprise in his voice, 'this is about halfway.'

'In time or altitude?'

'Both – yes, both.'

I was not greatly encouraged. After nearly three hours of climbing we still had another three hours to go, it seemed, and still half the Eiffel Tower to ascend. Furthermore, the rock face looked steeper to me, and even more unforgiving. We went around the Gendarme to the left and moved into a large gully under the south face. We were now out of the sun, but not sheltered from the wind that whistled through the gap between the Gendarme and the face above. It was bitterly cold.

This was the spot from which Mackinder, Ollier and Brocherel had moved around the amphitheatre above the Darwin Glacier, and then cut steps across the Diamond Glacier to the base of Batian. The Diamond Glacier hangs, literally hangs, from the ridge between Batian and Nelion, and is so steep that a man standing upright can easily cut steps at shoulder-height; a fall, unchecked, would take him over an ice-cliff and down on to the base of the Darwin Glacier, several hundred metres below. The glacial ice in which Mackinder and his companions were obliged to cut steps was exceptionally hard – hence the name Mackinder gave it, the Diamond Glacier; each step required 30 blows of the ice-axe, and the traverse on which they had expected to spend 20 minutes took a full three hours. They had left their overnight camp at 5.30 am, and finally reached the summit of Batian at noon. The summit was 'like a tower rising out of a heap of ruin ... A small platform a few feet lower adjoined the south-east corner of the crag, and from this I got two shots with my Kodak of the summit with César and Joseph upon it,' Mackinder reports. This photograph, often reproduced, is a fitting testimony to the two men about whom little is known, but who surely are due a good deal of the credit for Mackinder's success on Mount Kenya. Ollier was killed by a freak rockfall in the Alps while preparing for a chamois hunt in 1930, and his tombstone reputedly bears the inscription: 'Il est mort. Il n'est pas tombé' – 'He died. He did not fall.'

'We should go that way,' Thumbi suggested, pointing directly towards the head of the gully in which we had paused.

'Will that take us to De Graaf's Variation?' asked Iain.

'No, this is a more easy route. We go straight up to the notch, then round on to the face, and there is a way up from there,' Thumbi explained enthusiastically.

'I don't know that way. You're sure it's better than De Graaf's Variation?' Iain asked.

Thumbi Mathenge at the head of a traverse, ready to belay the next pitch.

Ropes used by Mackinder's party on the first ascent of Batian in 1899.

'Much better, yes. De Graaf's would take us two three hours, it is very difficult. This way is much easier.'

De Graaf's Variation is graded IV inferior – *very difficult* – so I rather favoured the allegedly easier alternative, especially since it would take us back on to the sunny side of the peak, while De Graaf's Variation would remain in the shade for some time yet.

While Iain tackled the pitch above, Thumbi stood on belay and I settled into a niche on the gully wall, but it offered little shelter from the freezing wind. A short length of hemp rope, whitened and frozen, hung from a cleft in the rock.

'Mackinder's,' Thumbi said, when I pointed it out to him. It was comforting to note that Mackinder's party had used fixed ropes on that part of the climb.

Iain did not find the route as straightforward as Thumbi had claimed it to be. He repeatedly asked for directions, and more than once requested confirmation that the route we were embarked upon was indeed easier than De Graaf's Variation. Thumbi of course replied that it was, but I began to wonder.

When Iain at last called out 'on belay' and offered the additional assurance that it was really nice to be back in the sunshine, he was out of sight beyond an imposing wall of rock.

'Take in!'

Horizontal and vertical fractures divided the rock into a series of blocks; all were very large, and few provided much in the way of foot- or handholds to assist the ascent from one to the next. The ropes pointed the way upward, through the comforting security of carabiners, but the wall looked very demanding to me. If this was the easy way, what was De Graaf's Variation like?

'Climbing!'

My progress was slow and physically demanding. On that pitch I recognized the importance of fingers in rock-climbing. I would reach up and feel over the rockface for a hold, and there were times when my hands seemed to follow an existence of their own. I remember watching them, and feeling quite detached, as they scrabbled about the rock like panic-stricken crabs seeking some nook, some cranny, some niche – something to hang on to: a hold! Just a centimetre or so would do. The fingers latched on to the merest ledge and the hands locked firm enough to support the entire body. One foot would rise until the edge of the sole slipped on to the ledge a hand had clung to not long before, then that foot would take the weight of the body, and the hands would move up to search for more holds.

It was desperately hard work, though the tension of clinging to a rock-face high on the mountain, freezing cold, eliminated most sensation of physical effort. Only when I arrived at a point where I could lean my elbows, at chest-height, on the next block I had to surmount, did I get some indication of the stress involved. And even then I watched as though it was happening to someone else. I was approaching the northern rib of Mackinder's Gendarme at the time; Iain was in sight, poised in the sunshine up to my left. An icy wind blew directly on to me through cracks in the rock above the ledge. I rested for a moment, and then the muscles of my right forearm cramped up. I can remember watching with intrigued curiosity as the fingers slowly clenched into the palm; then my left hand came into view and pulled the fingers straight again and massaged the forearm. Both hands were bleeding from several scratches. It was a bad moment. My progress immediately thereafter owed a lot to Iain's cheery exhortations, and I believe I also used the rope as a climbing aid more than is generally recommended.

When I finally reached the platform between the Gendarme and the main face, where Iain was belayed, I sat down and relaxed in the sunshine. When Thumbi joined us, it soon became apparent that Iain was not happy with our position.

'This is Windy Gap,' (it certainly was) 'Shipton's route. I didn't want to come this way.'

'But it is better than De Graaf's Variation, it's faster. De Graaf's could take two three hours, this will be much less.'

Iain was not convinced, but he followed Thumbi's directions without further complaint, moving round a bulge and out on to the face where it seemed to me there was only sheer rock and thin air.

'Dammit Thumbi!' he shouted back, 'this is Rickety Crack!'

'It's all right, the way is good,' Thumbi replied with a nervous laugh. 'It's much better than De Graaf's,' he said again.

I moved out to join Iain, and could well understand his reluctance to follow that route. I shared it absolutely. The Mountain Club Guide to Mount Kenya (edited by Iain Allan, as it happens) instructs climbers taking Shipton's route to get on to a small ledge at this point, and follow it to the right until it peters out on the main face. From there Rickety Crack leads upwards for about 8m. Shipton describes the position thus: '... I tried to the right and here found a narrow sloping ledge that led round a corner out of sight. It was an airy place above a sheer drop whose depth I did not bother to estimate. ... I found a shallow crack which split the surface of the wall above me. It was obviously the only line of possibility and I took it, though I was not at all happy. The crack was not wide enough to wedge my foot in it, and the only holds were smooth and sloping outwards. My progress was painfully slow, but soon the prospect of beating a retreat was even more repugnant than climbing on up.'

The ledge does peter out, exactly as the guide book describes, but I, for one, could see no feature on the smooth face that offered the remotest hope of further ascent.

'Up there,' Iain replied when I asked where the route led now. He pointed to a hump above the very end of the ledge. 'Rickety Crack is up there somewhere. This is the route Shipton and Wyn Harris took on the first ascent. Damn! I really didn't want to come this way!'

It was obvious that Iain was now in a state of controlled fury, and equally obvious that the cause was Thumbi's suggestion of an alternative route. Iain had not wanted to expose me to any more difficulty and danger than was absolutely necessary, and now we were perched on a tiny ledge, about to tackle Rickety Crack, a pitch that Shipton himself had found difficult and 'rather exposed'.

In mountaineering terminology, the word 'exposed' means open to danger. The ledge was certainly that. Little wider than the length of a boot at its widest point, and petering out to nothing just beyond, there was hardly room for the three of us to stand. As the ropes were re-coiled for the next pitch, and Thumbi prepared to stand on belay, Iain again protested that he had absolutely not wanted to take this route, and Thumbi again insisted than an ascent via De Graaf's Variation would have taken much longer. I was not sure whom to believe, which induced an unsettling state of mind. On the strength of Iain's annoyance, I did think of suggesting that we should return to the base of Mackinder's Gendarme and take the route he preferred; on the other hand, Thumbi seemed very confident, and the prospect of descending the pitch I had just climbed was not at all appealing. I decided to let fate take its course, and said nothing. At least the sun was still shining.

Eric Shipton and Percy Wyn Harris recorded the first ascent of Nelion on
the back of a cheque, which they cached on the summit.

Hall Tarns, the Temple and Lake Michaelson (centre) can be seen clearly
from the higher elevations of Nelion, when conditions permit.

Our perch afforded a fine view over the Lewis Glacier and down to the valleys beyond. I was delighted to catch sight of a line of climbers moving slowly up the ridge towards Point Lenana, and watched them with interest until the full implications of scale and elevation sank in. They were adults already standing above the height of Mont Blanc, yet from my position they looked like beetles crawling about where I would expect to see my foot when I lounge in a chair. And they probably could not even see us, I thought, remembering how difficult it had been to see Thumbi and his companions the day before. This shift of viewpoint brought a dramatic change of perspective to my own position. It was indeed a small and airy place that I occupied. The sheer rock of the south-east face on which we were perched extended to the right, above and below. Like Shipton, I did not bother to estimate the drop that fell away beneath my toes – in fact, I do not believe I so much as looked down. I was roped very firmly to a piton hammered in the rock at shoulder height, now I clung to it as well – with both hands, white-knuckled. Suddenly I realized that I was on the verge of becoming very frightened. One part of my mind retained an almost clinically objective attitude, observing that fear would not be helpful at this stage, but another, much deeper sensation threatened to overwhelm it. I knew then exactly how someone can become paralysed with fear, and began to imagine being stuck on the ledge, totally unable to move. This was the stuff of nightmares – such as those in which you are incapable of taking action to avoid a fearful threat, or are falling from a great height, falling … falling. Except of course, this was daytime, and there would be little hope of awakening after a fall from Rickety Crack.

The danger of petrified immobility came very close, but it was averted, I believe, firstly by a resurgent awareness that I was not only in the company of two men with vast experience of climbing on Mount Kenya, but also securely joined to them by lengths of sturdy rope, and secondly by a cheery call from above:

'On belay! It's all there, John. You just have to go for it!'

But first I had to change positions with Thumbi at the end of the narrowing ledge – a precarious manoeuvre in itself – before I could reach out to where the rope disappeared over the hump above. The fear had gone, and I remember feeling mildly surprised that in fact there were holds on the face, and that my fingers and toes were able to find purchase enough to support and raise the weight of my body. But it was fly-on-the-wall stuff. In due course I reached the crack – Rickety Crack – which Shipton had found too narrow for his boot, and the only holds smooth and outward-sloping. From some recess of memory, the stress of the moment flushed out a recollection of the hand-wedge strategy a friend had once described to me. You thrust your open hand as deep as possible into any suitable crack, then bring the thumb round on to the palm, he had said. The ball of the thumb then forms a wedge in the crack on which you can actually pull yourself upward. The idea had seemed laughable at the time, but I tried it on Rickety Crack – and it worked.

I was about two-thirds of the way up the crack when I lost my holds on the rock and slipped. My progress had been good to that point. The crack had opened-out to the width of my shoulders; horizontal fractures supplied finger- and toeholds; both feet and both hands were securely positioned, I thought. But then, as I pushed with my left leg and began raising my body in preparation for reaching up to higher handholds, my left foot slipped off the rock. With the weight thrown suddenly on to my right foot, that too slipped off, and in an instant I was hanging almost at arm's length. But just before I was obliged to test the strength of my fingerholds, there was a very comforting tug at the waist-belt of my harness. Iain was holding me, dangling as though from the top of a ten-storey building. I remember thinking that without the rope that would have been the end of the climb; my fingers would not have held. It was a very sobering moment, then, with adrenalin coursing through the system more powerfully than ever before, I quickly regained my footholds and literally surged up the remainder of the pitch to Iain's belay point. Neither of us so much as mentioned the slip (in fact we did not speak of it until we were off the mountain); I felt too numb, and Iain only muttered that he was getting tired of looking down and seeing the dead man beneath every belay. He wished the porters would hurry up and take the body away.

Eric Shipton described Rickety Crack as the key to the upper part of the mountain – 'the crux of the thing'. After that, it was 'an easy scramble all the way,' he said. An easy scramble for the likes of Eric Shipton, perhaps, though even lesser mortals like me have found that the success of climbing Rickety Crack certainly does tend to diminish the apparent difficulty of subsequent pitches. I recall no particular problems, though the Mountain Club guidebook tells me that in our ascent of the remaining 80m or so we scaled several pitches variously graded moderate to very difficult before reaching the col which overlooks the Diamond Glacier, and making the sharp right turn which leads over easy rock to the summit of Nelion. We arrived at noon – five hours after we had begun climbing.

5188m above sea level. The summit of Batian is just another 11m higher and only 140m away in horizontal distance, but getting there involves a difficult descent of more than 100m to the Gate of the Mists and then a scary hike across the topmost ridge of the Diamond Glacier – which falls away sharply on both sides. Scaling Batian adds another three hours to the ascent of Nelion, and this is the principal reason for Ian Howell's magnificent effort of erecting a small hut on Nelion. Climbers determined to stand on the top of Batian are advised to spend a night in the hut on Nelion. Iain offered me the opportunity of doing so, but I declined. It was not a difficult decision. Our ascent of Nelion was an honourable enough achievement, I thought.

We took some photographs on the summit, ate some nuts and raisins, drank some water and then prepared for the descent, which promised to be quite an adventure in itself, for much of it would be accomplished by abseiling – that is to say, using ropes to slide down the face of the peak – which was something I had not done before.

Iain seemed to regard the prospect of introducing me to the delights of abseiling, on the heights of Nelion, with amusement. Bemusement would be an accurate description of my state of mind as I watched Thumbi lead the way down – stepping backwards over the edge of the south-east face against a background of encroaching cloud and, far below, Lenana and the Lewis Glacier. At moments like that you are inclined to wonder about the breaking strain and age of the ropes, and how long do they last? (But I did not ask.) Nor can you prevent a rather awesome statistic from constantly returning to mind: of the 30 people who are known to have died in climbing accidents on the peaks since Shipton and Wyn Harris's first ascent of Nelion in 1929, all but six met their death on the descent, most while abseiling. I could understand why. Having reached the summit, you tend to feel that the difficult work is now done. Elation transforms tiredness into a mood of relaxed well-being and confidence. Mistakes are easily made when in that state of mind, and there is little margin for error on the descent from Mount Kenya's summits – particularly if you are sliding down ropes suspended from a single point of fixture.

Noon, 30 January 1988. The author on the summit of Nelion, photographed by Iain Allan.

Abseiling off Nelion, Lewis Tarn in the middle distance.

'Now John, this is as easy as …' Iain began as he prepared the ropes for my first attempt at abseiling, and I swear he was going to say 'as falling off a log', but recognized the unhappy connotation of that phrase in mid-delivery and changed the sentence so that it ended, rather lamely I thought, ' … as easy as anything.'

The rope was looped through a number of nylon slings fixed permanently to the rock at the rear of the platform on which we were standing, so that its two ends hung at equal length down the face. I was told that the fixture points are checked regularly, and new slings added if those already in place appear weak – which was reassuring. A stout aluminium device in the form of a figure 8 was attached to my harness, just below the navel, by means of a carabiner, the ropes were clipped into the carabiner as well, and a loop pushed up through the lower circle in the figure 8, down through the upper circle and then looped back over it. The ropes would slide through the device when allowed to do so, but friction would halt them whenever required, and the idea was that a climber would let the rope in with one hand, and out with the other, thus making a swift, controlled and elegant descent. When all parties were down, the rope would be pulled through the sling above and the next abseil prepared.

'You just have to stick your backside out over the edge as though you're sitting in a chair, and walk backwards down the face – you'll enjoy it,' Iain said.

Well, I'm not sure about that last assertion, though abseiling certainly is not a great deal more difficult than falling off a log. Iain gave me the additional security of a belay rope on the first two pitches, so that if I somehow managed to disengage the ropes, twist upside-down, or was reduced by fear to jibbering immobility, I would not fall or dangle unattended for too long, but could be lowered down to the ledge where Thumbi stood holding the ends of the abseil rope.

There is an element of wild adventure to abseiling. The very idea of sliding down a rope suspended from a high mountain is outrageous to the innate sensibilities of anyone accustomed to exercising the everyday caution needed to cross a busy street. In fact, to pursue the analogy a little farther, abseiling could be compared to walking backwards into the traffic on a one-way street – it's easy, exciting, and should not kill you.

On the mountain, you kick off from the ledge, let the rope into the 8-ring with one hand, and out with the other. If you can manage to coordinate the kicks off the rock with the slide of the rope you can abseil down speedily, in a series of bouncing leaps. However, the rope does heat up to an alarming degree as it passes through the rings; and beginners are apt to miss a kick, I found, and may occasionally twist around to find themselves swinging backwards into awkward corners of the face, where they may dangle, literally at a loose end, for short periods of time. Overhangs are also rather difficult to negotiate.

After the first two abseils, Iain suggested that I was now competent and confident enough to proceed without the belay rope. Then he could join the two ropes together, he explained, and we could abseil down a full rope-length – 50m – each time, and thereby speed up our descent appreciably. Though uncertain of both my competence and my confidence, the idea of leaving the mountain more rapidly was very appealing. It was mid-afternoon by then. Cloud was gathering around the peaks, bringing light flurries of snow, the temperature had fallen dramatically and the cruel face of the mountain was beginning to show through the veil of elation our ascent had drawn across it. I was cold, and felt drained by the physical and nervous tension of each abseil as I waited with Thumbi for Iain to descend.

The abseils did not follow the climbing route, but joined it occasionally, at the foot of a face, or at the head of a gully. While we waited for Iain, Thumbi would point out where we had climbed on the way up, if the route was in view, or else tell me about other features, other climbs. On a ledge at the foot of the main south face he said: 'This is where the man died. He was sitting there –' and he pointed to a narrow space where a man seated with his back against the rock would have had his legs dangling over the edge of a 30m cliff. The ledge was nowhere more than half-a-metre wide, and perhaps only three or four metres long; at its western end there was a small heap of human excrement and a strip of blue denim shirting which evidently had served as toilet paper. I felt intense sympathy for the dead man. Climbing mountains is generally supposed to be a spiritually liberating experience, but this was no place to die. Just a pile of rock, more lifeless, chilling and bleak than the most forsaken graveyard.

The ledge was at the head of a sheer cliff and the Darwin Glacier lay directly below, sloping steeply hundreds of metres down to the scree.

'This is the top of De Graaf's Variation?'

'Yes, the way is there,' Thumbi replied, pointing to a cleft at the eastern end of the ledge.

I peered over to look at the pitch he had described as so difficult, and could not agree that Windy Gap and Rickety Crack had afforded an easier ascent. But I could understand Thumbi's lack of enthusiasm for De Graaf's Variation.

We made seven abseils in all, each taking between 20 and 30 minutes, and climbed down several pitches as well. The descent took five hours, exactly as long as we had taken to reach the summit. The body had been taken away by then, but the ice-axe was still standing where I had left it against the rock at the foot of the climb – like a memorial cross, but more transitory, for Thumbi took it with him as we set off down the scree.

Down from the mountain, and evening cloud begins to fill the Teleki Valley.

Acknowledgements

Special thanks to Caroline Taggart, publisher, and Peter Campbell, designer, for their invaluable support and expertise.

I am also indebted to Perez Olindo, Director of Kenya National Parks, for his help; to Professor Godfrey Muriuki, the Hon. J.J.M. Nyagah, Monty Ruben, Philip Leakey, and Richard Leakey for their comments and advice; and to the Turner, Rainy, and Joyce households for their hospitality and logistical support.

On Mount Kenya itself I was helped generously and kindly by Livingstone Barine and his family, Lloyfor Mutegi, Steve Menja and a number of anonymous porters and rangers. My sincere thanks to all.

To the committee and members of The Mountain Club of Kenya, and to Iain Allan and Ian Howell in particular, I owe a very special debt of gratitude. Such unselfish and enthusiastic readiness to advise and help would be hard to match, and if the book is any good at all, the MCK deserves a large share of the credit. Thank you all, very much.

Cameras are good friends on a mountain trip – especially old and trusted cameras like the Nikons I kept warm in my sleeping bag each night on Mount Kenya. I carried two bodies and five lenses around the mountain. The F2 dates back to 1976, the FM to 1980; we've been on many trips together and they've never let me down. Most of the pictures were taken with either a 24mm wide-angle, or an 80–200 zoom; I used a 20mm for extra-wide scenes, a 35mm for the not-so-wide scenes and a 55mm micro took care of the close-ups – all Nikkor lenses.

Further Reading

On the history of Africa:

Clark, J.D. 1970. *The Prehistory of Africa.* Thames and Hudson, London.

Clark, J.D. and Brandt, S.A. (editors) 1984. *From Hunters to Farmers: the causes and consequences of food production in Africa.* University of California Press.

Ehret, C. and Posnansky, M. (editors) 1982. *The Archaeological and Linguistic Reconstruction of African History.* University of California Press.

McEvedy, C. 1980. *The Penguin Atlas of African History.* London.

Monod, T. (editor) 1975. *Pastoralism in Tropical Africa.* Oxford University Press.

Oliver, R. and Fage, J.D. 1988. *A Short History of Africa* (6th Edition). Penguin, London

Reader, J.A. 1988. *Missing Links: The hunt for earliest man.* Penguin, London.

On the history of East Africa and Kenya:

Beckwith, C. and Ole Saitoti, T. 1980. *Maasai.* Elm Tree/Hamish Hamilton, London.

Kenyatta, J. 1938. *Facing Mount Kenya.* Secker and Warburg, London.

Muriuki, G. 1974. *A History of the Kikuyu 1500 - 1900.* Oxford University Press, Nairobi.

Ogot, B.A. (editor) 1976. *Kenya Before 1900.* East African Publishing House, Nairobi.

Ogot, B.A and Kieran, J.A. (editors) 1968. *Zamani - A Survey of East African History.* East African Publishing House, Nairobi.

Phillipson, D.W. 1977. *The Later Prehistory of Eastern and Southern Africa.* Heinemann, London.

On Mount Kenya:

Allan, I. (editor) 1981. *Guide to Mount Kenya and Kilimanjaro.* Mountain Club of Kenya, Nairobi.

Benuzzi, F. 1952. *No picnic on Mount Kenya.* Kimber, London.

Dutton, E.A.T. 1929. *Kenya Mountain.* Cape, London.

Mackinder, H.J. 1900. *A Journey to the Summit of Mount Kenya.* Geographical Journal Vol 15 pp. 453–485, London.

Shipton, E.E. 1943. *Upon that Mountain.* Hodder and Stoughton, London.

Watteville, V. de, 1935. *Speak to the Earth.* Methuen, London.

Index